MUHAMMAD AL TIJANI AL SAMAWI

Then I Was Guided

Copyright © 1990 by Muhammad al Tijani al Samawi

All rights reserved. No part of this publication may be reproduced, stored or transmitted in any form or by any means, electronic, mechanical, photocopying, recording, scanning, or otherwise without written permission from the publisher. It is illegal to copy this book, post it to a website, or distribute it by any other means without permission.

First edition

Contents

Dedication	1
Foreword	3
A Brief Look at My Life	5
The Pilgrimage to the House of Allah	9
In Egypt	19
A Meeting on Board the Ship	23
My First Visit to Iraq	29
Abdul Qadir al-Jilani and Musa al-Kazim	31
Skepticism and Questioning	39
The Visit to al Najaf	45
A Meeting with the Al Ulama' (The Learned Men)	48
A Meeting with Al Sayyid Muhammad Baqir al Sadr	57
Skepticism and Perplexity	68
The Journey to Hijaz	75
The Beginning of the Research	87
The Companions of the Prophet as seen by the Shi'a and the...	90
The Companions at the Peace Treaty of al Hudaibiyah	96
The Companions and the Raziyat Yawm al Khamis (The Calamity...	100
The Companions in the Military Detachment under Usamah	107
The Opinion of the Quran regarding the Companions	122
The Opinion of the Messenger regarding the Companions	130
The Opinion of the Companions about Each Other	133
The Beginning of the Change	157
A Dialogue With a Scholar	159

The Reasons Behind the Enlightment	173
The Correct Prophetic Traditions Which Indicate the Fact...	194
Our Misfortune Regarding Ijtihad Against the Texts	214
An Invitation to Friends to Join the Research	225
The Guidance of Truth	230

Dedication

My book is a modest piece of work. It is a story of a journey ... a story of a new discovery, not a technical or natural discovery, but one in the field of religious and philosophical schools. Since any discovery is based primarily on a healthy mind and clear comprehension, which distinguishes human beings from all other creatures, I would like to dedicate this book to every healthy mind.

A mind which puts truth to the test and knows it from wrong, a mind which weighs all that has been said in the scale of justice, and always comes out in favor of reason.

A mind which compares words and sayings, and has the ability to distinguish between the logical and the not so logical, and between the strong and the feeble. Allah, the Most High, said,

"Those who listen to the saying and follow the best of it, those are guided by and they are the mindful."

To all of those I dedicate this book, hoping that Allah, Praise be to Him the Most High, opens our minds before our eyes, to guide us, to enlighten our hearts, to show us clearly the right way so we follow it, and to show us clearly the wrong way so we avoid it, and accepts us with His good servants, for He listens and He answers.

Muhammad al Tijani al Samawi

Foreword

In the Name of Allah, the Most Compassionate, the Most Merciful

Praise be to Allah, Lord of the Universe. He created man from clay and shaped him in the best possible way. He favored him above all other creatures and made His closest angels prostrate themselves before him. He graced him with the mind that changed his doubt to an absolute belief. He gave him two eyes, one tongue, two lips and showed him the two ways.

He sent him messengers giving him the good news, warning him, and alerting him, and preventing him from going astray with the cursed devil. He told him not to worship the Devil, for the Devil is his enemy, and to worship Allah alone and follow His right path, with understanding and a convincing belief, and not to imitate the belief of his forefathers and friends and relatives who followed those before them without any clear reasoning.

Who could say better things than he who called for Allah and did good deeds and said that he was one of the Muslims, may the Lord's blessings, peace and greetings be upon the Messenger who brought mercy unto the people, supporter of all the Oppressed and the weak, savior of all mankind from the darkness of ignorance, he who will guide them to the enlightened path of the faithful and the good.

Our master Muhammad ibn Abdullah, prophet of the Muslims, and chief of the singularly radiant may these blessings and greetings be upon his good and purified posterity whom Allah has chosen from among all the truthful. He stated in the Quran that we are compelled to love them, after he had purified them and made them infallible. He promised that anybody who goes on board their ship will be saved, and anybody who does not do so will perish.

May these blessings and greetings be upon his honorable companions who supported him, honored him and sacrificed themselves for him and for the victory of Islam. They knew the truth, so they pledged allegiance to him with conviction and stayed on the right path without changing it and were thankful. May Allah reward them for their services to Islam and the Muslims. May these blessings and greetings be upon their followers and upon those who kept on their path and were guided by their light to the Day of Judgment.

Please Lord accept my request for You are the All hearing and the Most Knowledgeable. Please my Lord open my heart for You are the One who guides us to the absolute truth.

Please my Lord help me to express myself, for you grant wisdom to any one You wish from amongst Your faithful worshippers. Please my Lord grant me more knowledge and join me with righteous people.

A Brief Look at My Life

I still remember how my father took me for the first time to the local mosque where al-Tarawih prayers were performed during the month of Ramadan. I was then ten years old. He introduced me to the men who could not hide their astonishment.

I knew previously that the tutor had arranged for me to perform al-Ishfa[1] prayers for two or three nights. It was customary for me to pray behind the man with some local children, and wait for the Imam to arrive at the second part of the Qur'an, i.e. Surat Meriam. My father made sure that we learnt the Qur'an at the Qur'anic school as well as at home through private lessons given to us by a blind man, who was related to us and who could recite the Qur'an by heart. Due to the fact that I learnt to recite the Qur'an at an early age, the tutor tried to show his good influence on me by teaching me the kneeling points in the recital. He tested me repeatedly to make sure that I had understood his instructions.

After I passed the test and finished performing the prayers and the recital, as well as I was expected to do, all the men came and congratulated me and my father, and thanked my tutor for his good efforts and blessings, and thanked Allah for Islam.

The memories of the days that followed are still with me today. I acquired so much admiration and my reputation went beyond our alley to the whole town. Those nights of Ramadan have left their religious marks on me to this day, and every time I go through an episode of confusion, I feel that there is a strange power which pulls me and puts me back on the path.

Every time I felt the weakness of the soul and the meaningless of life, these memories come to me to elevate me to a spiritual level and light in my conscience the flame of belief so that I can carry the responsibility. The responsibility which was given to me by my father, or more appropriately by my tutor, to lead the group in prayers at an early age made me feel as if I was not doing enough, or at least not up to the standard which was expected from me.

Therefore I spent my childhood and my adolescence in relative rectitude, but not without some innocent playing and an eagerness to know and to imitate. Throughout that period I was surrounded by the divine care which made me distinguishable amongst my brothers for my calmness and composure and for being on the right path and away from all immoral acts.

I should not forget to mention that my mother, may Allah bless her soul, had a big influence on me. She opened my eyes as she taught me the short chapters (surahs) of the holy Qur'an, the prayers and the rules of ritual purity. She took special care of me because I was her first son, and perhaps she found pleasure in educating me, as she was sharing the household with my father's first wife and her sons.

The name Tijani, which was given to me by my mother, has a special meaning in the al-Samawi family which had adopted the Tijani Sufi tariqa (order) ever since it was visited by a son of Shaykh Sidi Ahmed al-Tijani who came from Algeria. Many people of Gafsa - my family's home town - adopted the Tijani sufi order, especially the wealthy and educated families who helped to spread the order.

Because of my name, I became quite popular in the Samawi House and outside it, especially with those who were connected with the Tijani order. Therefore, many of the elders who were present at the above mentioned night during Ramadan came to congratulate my father and then kissed my head and hand and said, "These are the blessings of our master Shaykh Ahmad al-Tijani."

It is worth noting that the Tijani Sufi order is widely spread in Morocco, Algeria, Tunisia, Lybia, Sudan and Egypt, and those who believe in it are, somehow, fanatical about it. They do not visit the graves of other sages because, according to their belief, they acquired their knowledge from each other, whereas Shaykh Ahmed al-Tijani acquired his knowledge from the Messenger of Allah Muhammad (s.a.w.) directly, despite the fact that he came thirteen centuries after the Prophet (s.a.w.).

It has been said that Shaykh Ahmed al-Tijani used to communicate with the great Prophet (s.a.w.) by talking to him while he was awake and not in his sleep. Also it is believed that the complete prayers which were devised by the Shaykh are better than finishing the Holy Qur'an forty times.

In order to be brief I shall stop talking about the Tijani Sufi tariqa at this stage of the book, and if God wills it, I will refer to it elsewhere.

Thus I grew up with this belief, like any other youth in our town. We were all - praise be to Allah - Sunni Muslims following the teaching of Imam Malik ibn Anas, Imam of Dar al-Hijra. However, we, in North Africa, are divided in our Sufi orders. For example in Gasfa alone there are al- Tijaniyya, al-Qadiriyya, al-Rahmaniyya, al-Salamiyya and al-Isawiyya.

For each of the above orders, there are followers and supporters who could recite the order, poems and Dhikrs (invocation of God) in all special ceremonies such as weddings, circumcisions and vows. Apart from some negative aspects, these Sufi Tariqas played an important role in preserving the religious rites and in maintaining the respect for the sages.

Note

1. Al-Ishfa prayers, also called al-Tarawih, becase of the rest taken between every second prayer. Named "al-Ishfa"

The Pilgrimage to the House of Allah

I was eighteen years of age when the Tunisian national society of Scouts agreed to send me as one of six Tunisian representatives to the first conference for Islamic and Arab scouts which took place in Mecca. I was the youngest member of the mission, and certainly the least educated, for there were with me two headmasters, a teacher from the capital, a journalist and a fifth whose job I did not know, although I later realized that he was a relative of the then minister for education.

The journey was rather indirect, our first stop was Athens where we stayed for two days, next was Amman, the capital of Jordan, in which we spent four days, and then we arrived in Saudi Arabia and participated in the conference and performed the rites of pilgrimage and Umra.

I cannot describe my feelings when I entered the House of Allah for the first time; my heart was beating so fast. I felt as if it was coming out of my chest to see this ancient House for itself, and the tears kept coming out of my eyes endlessly. I imagined the angels carried me over the pilgrims and up to the roof of the Holy Kaba and answered the call of Allah from there: "Allah, here I am, your servant came to you to be at your service, Labbayka Allahumma Labbayk." Listening to other pilgrims, I gathered that most of them had waited for a long time and saved up throughout their lives to come to Mecca.

In my case, the journey was sudden and I was not prepared for it. I remember my father bidding me a tearful farewell, when he saw the airplane ticket and knew for certain that I was going to perform the Pilgrimage, saying, "Congratulations, my son, Allah has willed that you should perform the Pilgrimage before me at this age, for you are the son of Sidi Ahmed al- Tijani, pray for me at Allah's House to forgive me and grant me the pilgrimage to His House." I felt that Allah Himself called me and cared for me and brought me to the place where everybody longs to visit, although some cannot make it.

I appreciated this opportunity, therefore I threw myself into my prayers and tawaf (circling around the Kaba) even when the drinking from the water of Zamzam and going up the mountains where people competed to get to Hara cave in al-Nur mountain. I was only beaten by a young Sudanese pilgrim so I was "second of two". When I got there, I rolled myself on the floor as if I was rolling on the Great Prophet's lap and smelled his breathing what great memories they left such a deep impression on me that I will never forget.

Allah has cared for me in many ways, for I was liked by everybody I met in the conference, and many asked for my address in order to write to me in the future. As for my Tunisian companions, they looked down on me from the first meeting we had at the Tunisian Capital when we were preparing for the journey. I sensed their feeling, but I was patient, for I knew that the people of the North look down on the people from the South and consider them backward Soon enough their views started to change.

Throughout the journey and during the conference and the pilgrimage I proved myself to be worthy of their respect due to my knowledge of poetry and my winning of many prizes. I went back to my country with mare than twenty addresses from different nationalities.

We stayed twenty five days in Saudi Arabia, during which we met many learned Muslim scholars (Ulama) and listened to their lectures. I was influenced by some of the beliefs of the Wahabi sect and wished that all Muslims followed them. Indeed, I thought that they were chosen by Allah among all His worshippers to guard His House, for they were the purest and most knowledgeable people on earth, and Allah had given them oil so that they could serve and could care for the pilgrims, guests of the Merciful.

When I came back from the pilgrimage to my country I wore the Saudi national dress and was surprised by the reception that my father had prepared. Many people gathered at the station, led by Shaykhs of the Isawiyya, Tijaniyya and the Qadiriyya Sufi order complete with ceremonial drums.

They took me through the streets of our town chanting and cheering, and every time we passed a mosque I was stopped for a short time whilst people, especially the old folk, came to congratulate me with tears in their eyes longing to see the House of Allah and to visit the Prophet's grave. People looked at me as if they have not seen a young pilgrim (Hajj) of my age in Gafsa before.

I lived the happiest days of my life during that period, and many people, including the notables of the town came to visit and to congratulate me, and often asked me to read al-Fatihah (the Opening Sura of the Qur'an) with the prayers in the presence of my father, from whom I was embarrassed although he kept encouraging me. Every time a group of visitors left the house, my mother came to the sitting area to burn incense and read some amulets in order to rid me of bad spells.

My father kept the celebration going for three nights in the centre of the Tijani Sufi order, each night he slaughtered a sheep for a banquet. People asked me all sorts of questions, and my answers were mainly to praise the Saudis for their efforts to support and spread Islam.

Soon people started calling me Hajj (Pilgrim), and whenever somebody shouted Hajj, it only meant me. Gradually I became known amongst the various religious groups especially the Muslim Brotherhood, and I went around the mosques lecturing on religious issues, telling people not to kiss the graves or touch the woods for blessing because these are signs of Polytheism.

My activities started to increase and I was giving religious lessons on Fridays before the Imam's speech. I moved from Abi Yakub mosque to the Great Mosque because the Friday prayers were held in different times in those mosques; at midday in the former and during the afternoon in the latter.

On Sundays, my lessons were mostly attended by my students at the secondary school where I taught Technology. They liked me and appreciated my efforts because I gave them a lot of my time trying to help them in removing the clouds from their minds due to the teachings of the atheist and communist teachers of Philosophy and there were plenty of them!

My students used to wait with eagerness for these religious circles and some of them came to my house for I bought a number of Islamic books and read them thoroughly to bring myself up the standard of the questions I used to be asked. During the year in which I did the pilgrimage to Mecca, I completed the other half of my religious duties by getting married.

It was the wish of my mother to see me married before she passed away, for she had seen the weddings of all my half-brothers and Allah gave her what she wished and I got married to a young lady that I had never met before. My mother died after having been present at the birth of my first and second child, and she was preceded by my father who had died two years before her. Prior to his death he did the pilgrimage to Mecca, and two years later before his death, he turned to Allah in repentance.

The Libyan revolution succeeded during the period when the Arabs and the Muslims were feeling their humiliating defeat at the hands of the Israelis, and we saw that young revolutionary leader speaking on behalf of Islam and praying among his people calling for the liberation of al-Quds.

I became attracted to his ideas, as did many young Muslims and Arabs, and as a result we organized an educational visit to Libya by a group consisting of forty men for the Education Department. We visited the country at the beginning of the revolution and when we came back home we were very optimistic and hopeful for a better future for Muslims and Arabs in the whole world.

During the previous years I had corresponded with some friends, and my friendship with a few of them became very close, so that they even asked me to visit them. Thus, I made all the preparation for a journey during the summer vacation which lasted three months. I planned to go to Libya and Egypt by road and from there across the sea to Lebanon, Syria, Jordan and then to Saudi Arabia. I meant to do Umra there and to renew my commitment to the Wahabiyya in whose fervor I campaigned amongst the students and in the mosques which were frequented by the Muslim Brotherhood.

My reputation passed from my hometown to other neighboring towns through visitors who might attend the Friday prayer and listen to the lessons then go back to their communities. My reputation reached Shaykh Ismail al Hadifi, leader of the Sufi order in Tuzer, capital of al-Jarid and the birthplace of the famous poet Abu al-Qasim al-Shabbi. This Shaykh has many followers in Tunisia and abroad, especially among the working classes in France and Germany.

I received an invitation from him through his agents in Gafsa who wrote me a long letter thanking me fur my services to Islam and the Muslims. In the letter they claimed that the things I was doing would not bring me nearer to Allah because I had no learned Shaykh: "He who has no Shaykh his Shaykh will be a devil, and you need a Shaykh to show you the way, otherwise half of the knowledge is not completed." They informed me that (the greatest of his age) Shaykh Ismail himself had chosen me among all people to be one of his closest private circle of followers.

I was absolutely delighted when I heard the news. In fact I cried in response to the divine care which had elevated me to the highest and best places simply because I had been following the steps of Sidi al-Hadi al- Hafian, who was a Sufi Shaykh known for his miracles, and I had become one of his closest followers. Also I accompanied Sidi Silah Balsaih and Sidi al-Jilani and other contemporary Sufi leaders. So I waited eagerly for that meeting.

When I entered the Shaykh's house I looked curiously at the faces, and the place was full of followers among whom were Shaykhs wearing spotless white robes. After the greeting ceremony ended, Shaykh Ismail appeared and every one stood up and started kissing his hands with great respect. His deputy winked at me to tell me that this was the Shaykh, but I did not show any enthusiasms for I was waiting for something different from what I saw.

I had drawn an imaginary picture of him in my mind in accordance with what his agents and followers had told me about his miracles, and all I saw was an ordinary man without dignity or reverence. During the meeting I was introduced to him by his deputy, and the Shaykh received me warmly and sat me to his right and gave me some food.

After dinner the ritual ceremony started and the deputy introduced me again to take the oath from the Shaykh, and everybody congratulated me and blessed me. Later on I understood from what men were saying that I was known to them, which encouraged me to disagree with some of the answers given by the Shaykh to questions from the audience. Such behavior led some of the men to express their disgust and to consider it bad manners in the presence of the Shaykh who is usually left unchallenged. The Shaykh sensed the uneasy atmosphere and tried to cool the situation by using his wit, so he said,

"He whose start is burning, his end will be shining." The audience took that as a graceful sign from the Shaykh, which would guarantee my shining end, and congratulated me for that. However the Shaykh was clever and very experienced, so he did not let me continue with my irritable incursion and told us the following story:

One day a learned man attended a class held by a pious man and the pious man asked the learned man to go and get washed, so the learned man went and washed himself then returned to the class. The pious man repeated his demand, "Go and get washed". The learned man went and washed himself again thinking that he had not done it right the first time. When he came back to the class, the pious man asked him to wash again. The learned man started crying and said.

"Master, I have washed myself from my work and knowledge and I have nothing left except that which Allah has granted me through your hands." At that moment the pious man said, "Now you can sit down,"

I realized that I was the one whom the Shaykh referred to in the story, and everyone else realized that as well, for they rebuked me when the Shaykh left us to have a rest. They asked me to be silent and to show respect for the Shaykh lest I fail in my work, basing their argument on the Qur'anic verse:

> "O you who believe! Do not raise your voices above the voice of the Prophet, and do not speak loud to him as you speak to one another, lest your deeds become null while you do not perceive." (Holy Qur'an 49:2)

I then recognized my limits, so I complied and obeyed the orders, and the Shaykh kept me near him, and subsequently I stayed with him for three days, during which I asked him many questions, some of them to test his knowledge.

The Shaykh knew that and used to answer me by saying that there are two meanings for the Qur'an, one revealed and another hidden to a seventh degree. He opened his private safe for me and showed me a personal document which contained the names of pious and learned people connecting him with Imam 'Ali via many people such as Abu al-Hasan al- Shadhili.

It is worth noting here that these meetings held by the Shaykh are spiritual ones, and usually start with the Shaykh reciting and chanting some verses from the Qur'an. After that he reads a few poetic verses followed by chants and "dhikrs" by the men, and these chants are mainly centered on asceticism, piety and the renunciation of this life and the eagerness to seek the life hereafter.

After having finished with this part, the first man on the right hand side of the Shaykh reads what he can from the Qur'an, and when he says "And Allah said that truthfully" the Shaykh reads the beginning of another piece of poetry and the whole congregation recites it after him, each person then reading a Qur'anic verse. Shortly after that the men start leaning gently to the left and to the right, moving with the rhythms of the chants until the Shaykh stands up, and with him the entire congregation, forming a circle with him at the centre.

Next they start chanting Ah, Ah, Ah, Ah, and the Shaykh turns around in the centre, and then goes to each one of them, and shortly after that the tempo heats up and the men start jumping up and down, shouting in an organized but irritating rhythm.

After some hard work, quietness gradually prevails, and the Shaykh reads his last pieces of poetic verse, and then everybody comes to kiss the Shaykh's head and shoulders until they finally sit down. I have shared with those people in their rituals but not convincingly, for they contradicted my own beliefs of not attributing any associates to Allah i.e. not to request anything but from Allah. I fell on the floor crying and my mind scattered between two contradictory ideas.

One being the Sufi ideology in which a man goes through a spiritual experience based on the feeling of fear, on asceticism and on trying to approach Allah through the saints and the learned men.

The second idea was the Wahabi which had taught me that all of that was an attempt to attribute associates to Allah, and that Allah will never forgive them.

If the Great Prophet Muhammad (saw) cannot help, nor could he intercede, then what is the value of those saints and pious people who came after him?

In spite of the new position given to me by the Shaykh, for he appointed me as his deputy in Gafsa, I was not totally convinced, although I sometimes sympathized with the Sufi orders and felt that I should continue to respect them for the sake of those saints and God fearing people. I often argued, basing my argument on the Qur'anic verse:

"And call not with Allah any other god, there is no other god but He." (Holy Quran 28:88)

And if somebody said to me that Allah said:

"O you who believe be careful of (your duty to) Allah and seek means of nearness to Him." (Holy Quran 5:35)

I answered him quickly in the way that the Saudi Ulama had taught me by saying "The way to seek Allah is by doing a good deed." In any case, my mind was rather confused and troubled during that period, but from time to time some followers came to my house, where we celebrated al-Imarah (a type of dhikr).

Our neighbors felt uneasy about the noises which we produced, but could not confront me, therefore they complained to my wife, via their wives, and when I learnt about the problem, I asked the followers to celebrate dhikr elsewhere. I excused myself by informing them that I was going abroad for three months, so I said farewell to my family and friends and sought my God, depending on Him, and not believing in any other god but Him.

In Egypt

I stayed in Tripoli, the Libyan Capital, long enough to obtain an entry visa from the Egyptian Embassy to enter the land of Kinana i.e. Egypt. I met a few friends who helped me in this matter, so may Allah reward them for their effort. The road to Cairo is a long one, it took us three days and nights, during which I shared a taxi with four other Egyptians working in Libya who were on their way home.

Throughout the journey I chatted too them and read the Qur'an for them, so they liked me and asked me to be their guest in Egypt. I chose one of them, Ahmed. I felt very fond of him for he was a pious man and he gave me the highest level of hospitality. I stayed in Cairo twenty days during which I visited the singer Farid al-Atrash in his flat overlooking the Nile. I liked him for what I had read about his modesty in the Egyptian press, but I only managed to meet him for twenty minutes because he was on his way to fly to Lebanon.

I visited Shaykh Abdul Basit Muhammad Abdul Samad, the famous reciter of the Qur'an, whose voice I liked very much. I stayed with him for three days, and during that time I discussed with his friends and relatives many issues and they liked me for my enthusiasm, frankness and knowledge. If they talked about art, I sang; and if they spoke about asceticism and Sufism, I told them that I followed the Tijani order as well as the Medani; and if they spoke about the West I told them about Paris, London, Belgium, Holland, Italy and Spain which I visited during the summer holidays; and if they spoke about the pilgrimage, I told them that I had made the pilgrimage to Mecca and that I was on my way to perform the Umrah.

I told them about places which were not known to people who had been on pilgrimage seven times such as the caves of Hira and Thawr and the Altar of Ismail. If they spoke about sciences and technology I gave them all the figures and the scientific names; and if they spoke about politics, I told them my views saying, "May Allah bless the soul of al-Nasir Salah al-Din al- Ayyubi who deprived himself from smiling, and when some of his closest friends criticized him by saying: "The great Prophet (s.a.w.) was often seen smiling," he answered: "How do you want me to smile when the al-Aqsa Mosque is occupied by the enemies of Allah. Nay, by the name of Allah I will never smile until I liberate it or die."

Some of al-Azhar's Shaykhs used to come to these meetings and liked what I recited from the Qur'anic verses and the sayings of the Great Prophet Muhammad (s.a.w.), besides they were impressed by my strong arguments and asked me from which university I had graduated. I used to answer them proudly that I graduated from al-Zaituna University which was established before al-Azhar, and added, that the Fatimids - who established al-Azhar - started from the town of al-Mahdiah in Tunis.

I met many learned people in al-Azhar, and some of them presented me with a few books.

One day while I was at the office of an official responsible for the al- Azhar affairs, a member of the Egyptian Revolutionary Command Council came to attend a mass meeting for the Muslim and Coptic

Communities in one of the biggest Railway Companies in Cairo. The mass meeting was held in protest against Sabotage activities in the aftermath of the June war. The member of the Command Council insisted on my accompanying him to the meeting, so I accepted the invitation, and sat on the VIP rostrum between father Shnoodah and the Azhari Shaykh. I was also asked to address the meeting, which I did with ease due to my experience in giving lectures in Mosques and Cultural Committees in Tunis.

The main point which I have mentioned in this chapter is that I started feeling big and somehow over confident, and I thought I had actually become learned. Why should I not feel so when there were a number of Ulama from al-Azhar who attested for me, some of them even told me that my place was there, i.e. at al-Azhar. What really made me proud of myself was the fact that I was allowed to see some of the Great Prophet's (s.a.w.) relics.

An official from Sidi al-Husayn Mosque in Cairo took me to a room which could only be opened by himself. After we entered he locked it behind us, then he opened a chest and got the Great Prophet's (s.a.w.) shirt and showed it to me. I kissed the shirt, then he showed me other relics which belonged to the Prophet (s.a.w.), and when I came out of the room I cried and was touched by that personal gesture, especially when the official did not request any money from me, in fact he refused to take it when I offered it to him. In the end, and only after my insistence, he took a small amount and then he congratulated me for being one of those who have been honored by the grace of the Great Prophet (s.a.w.).

Perhaps that visit left a deep impression on me, and I thought for a few nights about what the Wahabis say regarding the Great Prophet (s.a.w.), and how he died and passed away like any other dead person. I did not like that idea and became convinced of its falsity, for if the

Martyr who gets killed fighting in the name of Allah is not dead but alive (by his God), then how about the master of the first and last. My feelings became clearer and stronger due to my early encounters with the teachings of the Sufis who give their Shaykhs and Saints full power to see to their affairs. They believe that only Allah could give them this power because they obeyed Him and accepted willingly what He offered them. Did He not state in the sacred saying: "My servant ... Obey me, then you will be like me, you order the thing to be, and it will be."

The struggle within me started to have its effect on me. By then I had come to the end of my stay in Egypt, but not before visiting, in the last few days, a number of mosques and I prayed in all of them. I visited the mosques of Malik, Abu Hanifah, al-Shafii, Ahmed ibn Hanbal, al-Sayyidah Zaynab and Sidi al-Husayn; I also visited the Zawiah of al-Tijani Sufi order, and I have many stories about the visits, some of them are long, but I prefer to be brief.

A Meeting on Board the Ship

I traveled to Alexandria on the exact day when there was an Egyptian ship on her way to Beirut. I felt exhausted both physically and mentally, so as soon as I got on the ship I went to bed and slept for two or three hours. I woke up when I heard a voice saying: "The brother seems to be tired." I replied positively and said: "The journey from Cairo to Alexandria made me feel so tired, because I wanted to be on time, so I did not have enough sleep last night."

I realized that the man was not Egyptian because of his accent, and I was, as usual, curious about him and eager to introduce myself to him. Apparently he was an Iraqi lecturer from the University of Baghdad and his name was Munim. He came to Cairo to submit his Ph.D. thesis at al-Azhar University.

We started our conversation by talking about Egypt and the Arab and the Muslim worlds, and we talked about the Arab defeat and the Jewish victory. The topics we covered through our conversation varied, and at one point I said that the reason behind the defeat was because of the divisions of the Arabs and Muslims into many small countries, so that despite the great number of their populations, their enemies do not pay any consideration to them.

We talked about Egypt and the Egyptians, and we both agreed about the reasons behind the defeat. I added that I was against these divisions which were emphasized by the colonial powers in order to facilitate our occupation and humiliation. I said that we even differentiated between the Hanafi and the Maliki and told him a sad story about an incident which happened to me in the "Abu Hanifah Mosque" in Cairo.

While I was there I prayed the afternoon prayer "al-Asr" with the men, and after we finished, the man standing next to me asked me with some anger, "Why did you not fold your hands in front of you during the prayers?" I replied with respect and courtesy that the Malikis prefer to drop their hands, and after all I am a Maliki. His reaction was: "Go to Maliki mosque and pray there." I left the mosque feeling disgusted and bitter, and I became even more perplexed.

The Iraqi teacher then smiled and told me that he was a Shi'i. I was a little disturbed by his answer and thoughtlessly said, "If I knew you were a Shi'i, I would not have spoken to you." He asked: "Why?" I replied, "Because you are not Muslims. You worship 'Ali ibn Abi Talib, and the moderates among you worship Allah but do not believe in the message of the prophet Muhammad (s.a.w.). You curse the Archangel Gabriel for betraying what he was entrusted with. Instead of delivering the message to 'Ali he gave it to Muhammad."

I continued with this type of anecdote while my companion listened carefully, at times smiling and at times showing his astonishment. When I finished talking, he asked me again, "Are you a teacher, teaching students?" I answered, "Yes." He said, "If that is what the teachers think, then we cannot blame the ordinary people who barely have any education."

I said, "What do you mean?" He answered, "I beg your pardon, but from where did you get all these false allegations?" I told him that my information came from famous history books, and the rest is common knowledge. Then he said, "Well let us leave the people, but could you tell me what books have you read?" I started mentioning a few books, such as those by Ahmed Amin "Fajr al-Islam, Duha al-Islam and Zuhor al-Islam" and many others.

He asked: "Since when has Ahmed Amin been an authority on the Shi'a?" He added, "To be fair and objective, one has to refer to the original sources of the subject." I said, "Why should I investigate a subject which is common knowledge to all people?" He replied, "Ahmed Amin himself has visited Iraq, and I was one of the teachers he met in Najaf, and when we rebuked him about what he had written about the Shi'a, he said that he was sorry, and he did not know anything about the Shi'a, and that was the first time he had met Shias. We told him that his excuse was worse than his mistake, for how could he write bad things about us when he did not know anything about us?"

He added, "Brother, if we judge the Jews and the Christians through the Holy Qur'an, they would not accept the judgment, despite the fact that the Qur'an is our absolute proof. Therefore, we should show their mistakes in their books, because then the proof would be stronger, in accordance to the saying: From among them, there was one who bore witness against them."

His speech fell on my heart like cold water falling on the heart of a thirsty man, and I changed from a bitter critic to someone who is willing to listen and think, because I felt there was a sound logic and a strong proof. So I had to show some modesty and listen to him. I said to him, "So you are one of those who believe in the message of our prophet Muhammad (s.a.w.)?" He replied, "All Shias like me believe in it. Brother, you had better investigate the matter yourself, so you do not have any doubt about your brothers the Shias, because perhaps some doubt is a sin."

He added, "If you really want to know the truth and to see it with your own eyes so you could convince yourself, then I invite you to visit Iraq, and there you will meet the Ulama of the Shi'a, as well as the ordinary people, and then you will recognize the malicious lies."

I said, "It has been my wish to visit Iraq one day to see its famous Islamic heritage, especially the Abbasid heritage, and in particular that of Harun al- Rashid. But, first of all, my financial resources are limited, and I have just enough to enable me to perform Umrah. Secondly, my present passport does not allow me to enter Iraq".

He replied: "Firstly, when I invited you to come to Iraq, that meant that I will take care of all your traveling costs between Beirut and Baghdad, both ways, and while you are in Iraq you will be staying with me, for you are my guest. Secondly, as far as the passport which does not allow you to enter Iraq, let us leave it to Allah, praise be to Him the Most High, and if Allah has decreed that you will visit, then it will be, even without a passport. However, we shall try to obtain an entry visa for you as soon as we arrive in Beirut".

I was very glad about that offer, and I promised my friend to answer his question the next day, if Allah the Most High willed it. I got out of the bedroom and onto the ship's deck breathing the fresh air, thinking seriously, while my mind was taken by the sea which filled the horizon. I thanked my God, Who created the universe, and who brought me to this place.

I asked Him, praise be to Him the Most High, to protect me from evil and the wicked and to guard me against errors and mistakes.

My mind wandered as I started to recall a series of events that I had experienced in the past. I remembered that happiness of my childhood up to that day and dreamed of a better future. I felt as if Allah and His Messenger were providing me with a special care. I looked towards Egypt, whose shores appeared from time to time on the horizon, and remembered how I had kissed the shirt of the Messenger of Allah (s.a.w.); they were my most precious memories of Egypt.

I recalled the words of the Shi'i which brought great joy to my heart, for it would fulfill an old dream of mine, that is to visit Iraq the country which reminded me of the court of al-Rashid and al-Mamun, who established Dar al-Hikmah which was sought by many students from the West in the days when the Islamic civilization was at its peak. In addition to that, it is the country of Shaykh Abdul Qadir al-Jilani, whose reputation had reached all countries, and whose Sufi order had entered every village a man whose high-mindedness surpassed everyone else's.

That, I thought, was another divine care from Allah to fulfill the dream. My mind wandered again until I was awoke by the sound of the loudspeaker calling the passengers to go to the canteen for their dinner, I made my way to the place but I found it was crowded with people, shouting and bustling as they were trying to enter it.

Suddenly, I felt the Shi'i pulling me by my shirt, saying: "Come here brother do not bother yourself, we will eat later without this crowd. In fact I looked for you everywhere." Then he asked me, "Have you prayed?" I answered, "No, I have not prayed yet." So he asked me to join him in his prayers and later to come and eat after all the hustle and bustle had gone.

I liked the idea, so I accompanied him to an isolated place where we did our ablution, and then I asked him to lead the prayers in front to test him and to see how he prayed, with the intention of doing my prayers later on. As soon as he called for the obligatory prayers at sunset and started reciting (Qur'anic verses) and reading various supplications, I changed my mind. I felt as if I was led by one of those pious and God fearing Companions of the Prophet, about whom I had read a lot. After he finished his prayers he read long supplications that I had not heard either in my country or in the countries I knew. I felt at ease every time I heard him praising the Prophet Muhammad (s.a.w.) and his family and giving them what they rightly deserve.

After the prayers I noticed tears in his eyes, also I heard him asking Allah to open my eyes and to lead me to the right direction.

We went to the canteen which was almost empty, and he did not sit down until I had sat down, and when they brought us the food, he changed his dish for mine because his had more meat than mine.

He treated me as if I was his guest and kept telling me stories that I had never heard before concerning food, drink and table manners. I liked his manners. He led the evening prayers and extended it by reciting long supplications until I started crying, then I asked Allah, praise be to Him, to change my suspicions about the man because "Some doubt might be a sin." But who knows?

I slept that night dreaming about Iraq and the Arabian Nights, and I was woken by my friend calling the dawn prayers. We prayed together, then sat and talked about Allah's graces on the Muslims. We went back to sleep and when I got up again I found him sitting on his bed with a rosary in his hand mentioning the name of Allah, so I felt more at ease with him, and asked my God for forgiveness.

We were having our lunch in the canteen when we heard from the loudspeaker that the ship was approaching the Lebanese shores, and with Allah's help, we would be in Beirut harbor in two hours time. He asked me if I had thought about the matter, and what I had decided. I told him if Allah willed it and I got an entry visa, then I did not see why not, and I thanked him for his invitation.

We arrived in Beirut, where we spent one night then we left for Damascus.

As soon as we got to Damascus we went to the Iraqi Embassy there and obtained a visa at incredible speed. When we left the Embassy he congratulated me, and we thanked Allah for His help.

My First Visit to Iraq

We left Damascus for Baghdad in one of the al-Najaf International Company coaches.

When we arrived in Baghdad, where the temperature was 40 degrees, we went to the Jamilah quarter in the district of al-Ummal, and entered my friend's airconditioned house. We had a rest, and then he brought me a long shirt called Dishdasha. Some fruit and food were also brought for me. Then members of his family came to greet me with respect and politeness, and his father embraced me as if we had known each other before.

As for my friend's mother, who stood at the door wearing a long black coat, she also greeted me and welcomed me. My friend apologized on behalf of his mother who could not shake my hands, because it was not permitted. I liked their manners and said to myself, "These people whom we accused of being deviants seem to observe the religion more than us."

During the days of our travel together I sensed in my friend his noble manners, his self-esteem and his generosity. I also sensed in him modesty and piousness that I had never experienced with anybody else before. I felt that I was not a stranger, but as if I was at home.

When darkness fell, we went up on the roof of the house where there were some beds prepared for us. I could not go to sleep easily for I was in a state of delirium: Was I really in Baghdad next to Sidi Abdul Qadir al- Jilani? My friend laughed as he asked me what the Tunisian people think of Abdul Qadir al-Jilani.

I started telling him about the miracles which are attributed to him, and all the places which are established and named after him. I told him that he is the "Centre of the circle", and as Muhammad the Messenger of Allah is the master of all the prophets, Abdul Qadir is the master of all the saints. His feet are on the necks of all the saints, and it was him who said, "Everyone goes round the house seven times, and I will go around the house with my tents."

I tried to convince him that Shaykh Abdul Qadir came to see his followers and treat them if they were ill and comfort them if they were depressed. I might have forgotten the influence of the Wahabi ideas on me, which state that all of that is polytheism. When I noticed the lack of enthusiasm in my friend, I tried to convince myself that all of what I have said was not right. I also asked him about his opinion.

My friend laughed and said, "Tonight have a good sleep and rest your tired body, and tomorrow, if Allah wills it, we will go and visit the grave of Shaykh Abdul Qadir."

I was absolutely delighted with the news and wished it was dawn then. I was so tired that I went into a deep sleep and did not get up until the sun was shining on me. I missed my prayer, and my friend told me that he tried several times to wake me up but without success, so he left me to rest.

Abdul Qadir al-Jilani and Musa al-Kazim

After breakfast we went to Bab al-Shaykh and saw the place that I had always wished to visit. I ran to enter the place like a man who was eager to see him and to throw myself on his lap.

I mixed with the multitude of visitors who were gathering around the place like the pilgrims in the House of Allah. Some of the visitors were throwing sweets, so I quickly picked up two. I ate one for blessing and kept the other in my pocket as a souvenir. I prayed there, recited some supplications and drank water as if I was drinking from Zamzam.

I asked my friend to wait for me until I wrote a few postcards to my friends in Tunisia to show them the picture of the place of Shaykh Abdul Qadir with its green dome. I wanted to prove to my friends and relatives in Tunisia my high state which brought me to this place that they have never been able to reach.

We had our lunch in a popular restaurant in the middle of the capital, and then I was taken by my friend to a place called al-Kazimiyyah. I only got to know that name through him mentioning it to the taxi driver who took us there.

When we arrived in al-Kazimiyyah we joined a multitude of people, children, men and women walking in the same direction. Everyone was carrying something with him or her, which reminded me of the time of the pilgrimage. I did not know where they were going until I noticed a glittering coming from golden domes and minarets. I understood that it was a Shi'a mosque, because I knew before that they decorate their mosques with gold and silver; something Islam has prohibited. I did not feel at ease when we entered the mosque, but I had to respect my friend's feelings and follow him without choice.

When we entered the first door I noticed that some old people were touching it and kissing it, so I engaged myself with reading a plaque saying: "Unveiled Ladies are not allowed to enter", with a saying by Imam 'Ali: "A day will come when women are seen wearing transparent clothes or even naked...etc."

When we reached the shrines, my friend started reading the permission to enter, while I occupied myself by looking at the gate and I was astonished by all the gold and engravings of the Qur'anic verses which covered that gate. My friend entered first then I followed him, and my mind was full of the legends and fables which I had read in books which condemn the Shi'a. Inside the shrine I saw engravings and decorations that I have never seen before, and I was surprised by them and felt as if I was in an unknown and unfamiliar world.

From time to time I looked with disgust at those people who were going around the grave, crying and kissing its bars and corners, while others were praying near the grave. At that moment a tradition of the Prophet Muhammad (s.a.w.) came to my mind, which states: "Allah cursed the Jews and Christians for making mosques of the graves of their saints." I walked away from my friend, who, as soon as he entered, started crying, and left him to do his prayers.

I approached the plaque which was written especially for the visitors and read it but could not understand most of it because it contained strange names that I did not know. I went to a corner and read the

Opening Surah of the Qur'an (al-Fatiha) and asked Allah for mercy on the person who is inside the grave saying: "O Allah if this dead person is a Muslim then have mercy on him for You know him better than I do."

My friend came near me and whispered in my ears, "If you want anything you better ask Allah in this place because we call it the gate of requests." I did not pay much attention to what he said. God forgive me, rather, I was looking at the old men with black or white turbans on their heads and the signs of prostration on their foreheads, with their long perfumed beards, which added to their dignity alongside their awesome looks.

I noticed that as soon as one of them entered the shrine, he started crying, and I asked myself, "Is it possible that all these tears are false? Is it possible that all these old people are wrong?"

I came out perplexed and astonished about what I had seen, while my friend walked backwards, as a sign of respect, so that he did not turn his back to the shrine.

I asked him, "Whose shrine is that?" He said, "Imam Musa al-Kazim." I asked, "Who is Musa al-Kazim?" He said, "Praise Allah! You, our brothers, of the Sunni sect ignored the essence and kept the shell."

I answered him angrily, "What do you mean we ignored the essence and kept the shell?"

He calmed me down and said, "My brother, since you came to Iraq you never stopped talking about Abdul Qadir al-Jilani, but who is Abdul Qadir al-Jilani, and why should he attract all your attention?"

I immediately replied proudly, "He is one of the descendants of the Prophet. And had there been a prophet after Muhammad it would have been Abdul Qadir al-Jilani, may Allah be pleased with him." He said, "Brother al- Samawi, do you know Islamic history?"

I answered without hesitation, "Yes." In fact what I knew of Islamic history was very little because our teachers prevented us from learning it, for they claimed that it was a black history, and not worth reading. I remember, for example, when our Arabic Rhetoric teacher was teaching the Shaqshaqiyyah oration from the book "Nahj al-Balaghah" by Imam 'Ali, that I was puzzled, as were many other students, when we read it, but I dared to ask the following question: "Are these truly the words of Imam 'Ali?"

He answered: "Definitely, who would have had this eloquence apart from him. If it were not his saying, why should the Muslim scholars like Shaykh Muhammad Abduh, the Mufti of Egypt, concern themselves with its interpretation?" Then I said, "Imam 'Ali accuses Abu Bakr and Umar that they robbed him of his right to succeed as Caliph."

The teacher was outraged and he rebuked me very strongly and threatened to expel me from the class, and added, "We teach Arabic Rhetoric and not history. We are not concerned with the dark episodes of history and its bloody wars between Muslims, and in as much as Allah has cleaned our swords from their blood; let us clean our tongues by not condemning them."

I was not satisfied with the reasoning, and remained indignant towards that teacher who was teaching us Arabic Rhetoric without meaning. I tried on many occasions to study Islamic history but I did not have enough references nor the ability to buy books. Also I did not find any of our learned people to be interested in the subject, and it seemed to me as if all of them had agreed to forget all about it and not to look into the matter. Therefore, there was no one who had a complete history book.

When my friend asked me about my knowledge in history, I just wanted to oppose him, so I answered him positively, but it was as if I was saying, "It is a dark history, full of civil strives, intrigues and contradictions." He said, "Do you know when Abdul Qadir al-Jilani was born?" I answered, "Approximately between the sixth and the seventh century."

He said, "How many centuries then have elapsed between him and the Messenger of Allah?" I said, "six centuries." He said, "If there are two generations in a century then there were at least twelve generations between Abdul Qadir al-Jilani and the Messenger."

I agreed. Then he said, "This is Musa ibn Jafar ibn Muhammad ibn 'Ali ibn al-Husayn ibn Fatima al-Zahra, between him and his great-great-great grandfather, the Messenger of Allah, there were only four generations. In fact he was born in the second Hijra century, so, who is nearer to the Messenger of Allah, Musa or Abdul Qadir?"

Without thinking I said, "Him of course. But why don't we know him or hear people refer to him?"

He said, "This is the point, and that is why I said, and allow me to repeat it, that you have ignored the essence and kept the shell, so please do not blame me and I beg your pardon."

We talked and talked, and from time to time we stopped until we reached a learning place where there were teachers and students discussing ideas and theories. As we sat there I noticed my friend started looking for somebody, as if he had prior appointment.

A man came towards us and greeted us then started talking with my friend, and from the conversation I understood that they were colleagues at the university, and that another colleague was coming to the place soon. My friend said to me, "I brought you to this place to introduce you to a historian scholar, who is a professor of history at the University of Baghdad, and his Ph.D. thesis was about Abdul Qadir al-Jilani and he will be of use to you, with the help of Allah, because I am not a specialist in history."

We drank some cold juice until the historian arrived, and I was introduced to him, then my friend asked him to give me a brief historical view on Abdul Qadir al- Jilani. After we had more cold drinks, the historian asked me questions about myself, my country and my job and asked me to talk to him about the reputation of Abdul

Qadir al-Jilani in Tunis.

I gave him plenty of information in this field and told him that people think that Abdul Qadir carried the Messenger of Allah on his neck during the night of Mi'raj (the night of the prophet Muhammad's (s.a.w.) ascension to the seven heavens) when Gabriel was late for fear of getting burnt. The

Messenger of Allah told him then, "My foot is on your neck and your foot will be on the neck of all the saints until the Day of Judgment."

The historian laughed when he heard what I said, but I did not know whether he laughed at those stories or at the Tunisian teacher standing in front of him!

After a short discussion about the saints and the pious people, he told me that he had researched for seven years, during which he traveled to Lahore in Pakistan, Turkey, Egypt, Britain and to all the places where there are manuscripts attributed to Abdul Qadir al-Jilani and he scrutinized them and photographed them but could not find any proof indicating that Abdul Qadir al-Jilani was a descendant of the Messenger. All what he found was a verse attributed to one of his offspring in which he says, "...and my forefather was the Messenger of Allah."

It was perhaps the interpretation of some of the learned people of the saying of the Prophet "I am the grandfather (forefather) of every pious person." He also informed me that recent historical research proved that Abdul Qadir al-Jilani was not an Arab but of a Persian origin, and came from a small town in Iran called Jilan, and he moved to Baghdad where he studied and then taught at a time when there was a moral decay. He was a God-fearing man and people liked him, so when he died they established the Qadiriyyah sufi order in his memory, as was the case with the followers of any Sufi teacher. He added, "Truly, the Arabs are in a lamentable state with regard to this situation."

A Wahabi rage stormed in my mind and I said, "Therefore, Doctor, you are a Wahabi in ideology, for they believe in what you are saying, there are no saints." He said, "No, I am not a follower of the Wahabi ideology. It is regretful that the Muslims tend to exaggerate and take extreme views. They either believe in all the legends and fables which are not based on logic or canonical law, or they deny everything, even the miracles of our Prophet Muhammad (s.a.w.) and his sayings because they do not suit their way of thinking."

For example, the Sufis believe in the possibility of Shaykh Abdul Qadir al-Jilani being present in, let us say, Baghdad and Tunis at the same time; he could cure a sick man in Tunis and simultaneously rescue a drowning man in the River Tigris in Baghdad. This is an exaggeration. As a reaction to the Sufi thinking, the Wahabis denied everything, and they said that even the pleading to the Prophet is polytheism, and this is negligence. No my brother! We are as Allah said in His Glorious Book:

"And thus we have made you a medium (just) nation that you may be the bearers of witness to the people." (Holy Qur'an 2:143)

I liked what he had said very much, and thanked him for it. I also expressed some conviction in his argument. He opened his briefcase and got his book on Abdul Qadir al-Jilani and gave it to me as a present. He then invited me to his house but I excused myself, so we talked about Tunis and North Africa until my friend came back and then we returned home after having spent the whole day visiting friends and holding discussions.

I felt tired and exhausted, so I went to sleep. I got up early in the morning and started reading the book which dealt with the life of Abdul Qadir, and by the time my friend got up I had finished half of the book. He asked me several times to have my breakfast, but I refused until I had finished the book. I became attached to the book which put me in a state of skepticism which lasted until just before I left Iraq.

Skepticism and Questioning

I stayed in my friend's house for three days, during which I had a rest and thought carefully about what I had heard from these people whom I had encountered and who appeared to me as if they were living on the moon. Why had people always told us nasty things about them, and why should I hate them and despise them without knowing them?

Perhaps all this had come from the rumors we hear about them that they worship 'Ali, and that they view their Imams as gods and believe in reincarnation, and worship stones rather than Allah, and they - as my father had told me after he came back from pilgrimage - came to the Prophet's grave to throw dirt on it, and were caught by the Saudis who sentenced them to death etc.

After hearing all that, it is not surprising that other Muslims hate and despise, even fight the Shi'a.

But how could I believe these rumors after all I had seen with my eyes and heard with my ears.

I spent over a week amongst these people and I did not see or hear from them anything that is not compatible with logic. In fact I liked the way they worshipped, I liked their prayers, their manners, and the respect they gave to their learned people, and wished that I could be one of them. I kept asking myself, "Is it true they hate the Messenger of Allah, and every time I mentioned his name, and often I did that just to test them, they shouted from the heart "May Allah bless Muhammad and his household"?

At the beginning I thought they were hypocrites, but later I changed my mind, especially after I read some of their books in which I found a great deal of respect and veneration for the Messenger which I have never found in our books. For example, they believe in the absolute infallibility of the Prophet Muhammad (saw), before and after his mission.

Whereas we, the Sunnis, believe in his infallibility in delivering the Qur'an only, and apart from that he was just another human being, subject to committing mistakes. We have many examples to show that the Prophet was wrong and that he was corrected by his Companions. The Shi'a refuse to accept the fallibility of the Prophet while others were correct. So after that, how could I believe that they hate the Messenger of Allah? How could I? One day while I was talking to my friend I asked him to answer me frankly, and the following dialogue took place:

- You place 'Ali, may Allah be please with him, and may He honour him, at the same level as the prophets, because whenever I hear his name mentioned you say "Peace be on him".
- That is right whenever we mention the name of the Commander of the Faithful (Imam 'Ali or one of the Imams of his off-spring we say "Peace be upon him", but this does not mean that they are prophets. However, they are the descendants of the Prophet, and Allah has ordered us to pray for them, therefore we are allowed to say "May Allah bless them and grant them peace" as well.
- No brother, we do not say "May Allah bless him and grant

him peace" except on the Prophet Muhammad (saw) and on the Prophets who came before him, and there is nothing to do with 'Ali or his descendants, may Allah be pleased with them all, in this matter.
- I would like to ask you to read more, so that you know the truth.
- Brother, which books should I read? Is it not you who told me that the books of Ahmed Amin are not the authoritative books on the Shi'a, in the meantime the Shi'a's hooks are not the authoritative books on us and we do not rely on them. Do you not see that the Christians' hooks which they refer to, state that Jesus said, "I am the son of Allah" while the Glorious Qur'an, which says the absolute truth, quotes Jesus saying:

"I did not say anything to them except what you have ordered me to do, and that is to worship Allah, my God and your God." (Holy Qur'an 5:117)

- Well said! I did say that. What I want from you is this, to use one's mind and logic and to base one's argument on the Glorious Qur'an and the correct Sunna (the Prophet Muhammad's (saw) tradition) as long as we are Muslims, and if we were talking to a Jew or Christian then we would have based our argument on something else.
- Well, in which book will I find the truth? Every writer, every group and every creed claims to be the right one.
- I will give you tangible evidence which is agreed on by all Muslims regardless of their creed or group, but you do not know it.
- Say, God, grant me more knowledge.
- Have you read the commentary on the following Qur'anic verse:

"Surely Allah and His angels bless the Prophet. O you who

believe call for (Divine) blessing on him and salute him always" (Holy Qur'an 33:56).

All the commentators, Shi'a and Sunnis, agreed that the Companions of the Prophet, about whom the above Qur'anic verse was revealed, cared to see the Prophet and said, "O Messenger of Allah we know how to salute you, but we do not know how to pray on you."

He said. "Say, may Allah bless Muhammad and the household of Muhammad in the same way as you bless Ibrahim and the household of Ibrahim in the world, You are the Praise-worthy and the Glorious, and do not pray on me by the shortened (al-Batra') prayer." They said, "And what is the shortened prayer, O Messenger of Allah?" He said, "Why do you say may Allah bless Muhammad and then stop, for Allah is perfect and only accepts perfection." After that the Prophet's companions followed the Prophet's order and they performed the complete prayer.

Even Imam al-Shafii said in their honour:

"O household of the Messenger of Allah Your love is an order from Allah revealed in the Qur'an You are highly honored, and he who does not bless you, his prayer is not valid.

I listened very carefully to what he had said, and his words entered my heart and found a positive echo."

Indeed, I had read what he had said in some books but could not remember their titles, and confessed to him that when we say our blessings on the Prophet we also include all his household and Companions, but we do not specify 'Ali with the salutation, as the Shi'a do.

He asked, "What do you think of al-Bukhari?"

I said, "He is a great Sunni Imam and his book is the most reliable book after the book of Allah (the Qur'an)." Then, he stood up and pulled "Sahih al-Bukhari" from his library and searched for a particular page he wanted and gave it to read: "We have been informed by so and so that 'Ali (may Allah grant him peace) ..."

I could not believe my eyes and was very surprised to the extent that I thought it was not "Sahih al-Bukhari", and looked at the page and the cover again, and when my friend sensed my doubtful looks, he took the book from me and opened another page, it read: "'Ali ibn al-Husain, may Allah grant them peace." After that I could only say to him, "Glory be to Allah." He was satisfied with my answer, so he left the room and I stayed behind thinking, reading those pages again and making sure of the book's edition, which I found had been published and distributed by al-Halabi & Sons Co. in Egypt.

- O my God, why should I be so arrogant and stubborn, for he gave me a tangible reasoning, based on one of our most reliable books, and al-Bukhari was not Shi'i at all, in fact he was a Sunni Imam and scholar.

Should I submit to them regarding the fact that 'Ali is worthy of the title "may Allah grant him peace", but I am afraid of this fact, since it might bring other subsequent facts that I do like to admit to. I was beaten twice by my friend, the first time when I accepted the non-holiness of Abdul Qadir al-Jilani, the second when I accepted that Musa al-Kazim was more important than him (i.e. al-Jilani).

Furthermore, I agreed that 'Ali was worthy of the title "may Allah grant him peace", but I did not want another defeat, for only days before I was proud of myself for being considered a learned man in Egypt and the scholars of al-Azhar were praising me. Today I find myself beaten and defeated, and by whom? By those whom I had thought, and still thought, were wrong, and I have always used the word "Shi'a" as a swear word.

It is arrogance and selfishness, it is stubbornness and bigotry, please God grant me forth rightness and help me to accept the truth even if it is bitter, God open my eyes and grant me insight and lead me on Your path and make me one of those who listen to the sayings and follow the best.

God show us the right as right and grant us the ability to follow it; and show us the wrong as wrong and grant us the ability to avoid it.

I went back home with my friend and continued to say these pleas, so he said with a smile,

> *"May Allah lead us and you and all Muslims to the right path, and He said in His Book: 'And (as for) those who strive hard for Us, We will most certainly guide them in Our ways, and Allah is most surely with the doers of good.'" (Holy Quran 29:69)*

The word strive (Jihad) in the Qur'anic verse carries the meaning of scientific research to reach the truth, and Allah will lead anyone to the truth, if he chooses to seek it.

The Visit to al Najaf

One night my friend told me that we were going on the next day, if Allah willed, to al-Najaf. I asked him, "What is al-Najaf?" He said, "It is a centre for learning, also the grave of 'Ali ibn Abi Talib is in that city."

I was surprised that there was a known grave for Imam 'Ali, for all our Shaykhs say that there is no known grave for our master 'Ali. We took a bus to al-Kufa and there we stopped to visit al-Kufa Mosque, which is one of the most celebrated Islamic monuments. My friend showed me all the historical places and took me to the mosque of Muslim ibn Aqeel and Hani ibn Urwa and told me briefly how they were martyred. He took me to the Mihrab where Imam 'Ali was martyred, then we visited the house where the Imam lived with his two sons, our masters al-Hasan and al-Husayn, and in the house there was a well from which they drank and did their ablution.

I lived some spiritual moments during which I forgot the world and imagined the asceticism and the modesty of the Imam, despite the fact that he was Commander of the Believers and fourth of the Rightly Guided Caliphs.

I must not forget to mention the hospitality and the modesty of the people of al-Kufa, since whenever we passed a group of people they stood up and greeted us, as if my friend knew most of them. One of those we met was the director of the Institute of al-Kufa, who invited us to his house where we met his children and spent a happy night. I had the feeling that I was amongst my family and my clan, and when they talked about the Sunnis they always said, "Our brothers from the Sunna", so I liked their talks and asked them a few questions to test their sincerity.

We continued our journey to al-Najaf, some ten kilometers from al-Kufa, and when we got there I remembered al-Kazimiyyah mosque in Baghdad, for there were golden minarets surrounding a dome made of pure gold. We entered into the Imam's mausoleum after having read a special reading for permission to enter the place, which is customary amongst the Shi'a visitors. Inside the mausoleum I saw more surprising things than that in the mosque of Musa al-Kazim, and as usual, I stood and read al-Fatiha, doubting whether the grave actually contained the body of Imam 'Ali. The simplicity of that house in al-Kufa which was occupied by the Imam had impressed me very much to the extent that I thought, "God forbid, Imam 'Ali would not accept all this gold and silver decoration, when there are many Muslims dying of hunger all over the world."

Especially when I saw many poor people lying on the streets asking for alms. Then I said to myself, "O Shi'a, you are wrong, at least you should admit this mistake, for Imam 'Ali was sent by the Messenger of Allah to demolish the graves, so what are all these gold and silver graves, if this is not polytheism then it must be at least an error that Islam does not allow."

My friend asked me as he handed me a piece of dry clay if I wanted to pray. I answered him sharply, "We do not pray around the graves." He then said, "Wait for me until I do my prayers." While I was waiting for him I read the plaque which hung on the grave, I also looked inside it through the engraved gold and silver bars and saw many coins and notes of different denominations thrown by the visitors as contributions to the charitable works which are attached to the mausoleum.

Because of the vast quantity of money, I thought it might have been left there for months, but my friend told me that the authorities responsible for cleaning the place collect the money every night after the evening prayer.

I went out after my friend, astonished by what I had just seen, and wished that they would give me some of that money, or perhaps distribute it among the many poor people. I looked around the place, which was surrounded by a great wall, and saw many groups praying here and there, others were listening to speakers standing on platforms, some of them sounded as if they were wailing.

I saw a group of people crying and beating their chests, and I wanted to ask my friend why should these people behave in such a way, but a funeral procession passed by us and I noticed some men removing a marble flag from the middle of the great courtyard to lower the body there. Therefore I thought that these people were crying for their lost one.

A Meeting with the Al Ulama' (The Learned Men)

My friend took me to a mosque next to the mausoleum, where the floors were covered by carpets, and around its Mihrab there were some Qur'anic verses, engraved in beautiful calligraphy. I noticed a few turbaned youngsters sitting near the Mihrab studying, and each one of them had a book in his hand.

I was impressed by the scene, since I had never seen Shaykhs aged between thirteen and sixteen, and what made them look so cute were their costumes. My friend asked them about the Master "al-Sayyid", so they told him that he was leading the prayer. I did not know what he meant by "al- Sayyid", and thought he might be one of the Ulama, but later I realized it was "al-Sayyid al-Khu'i" the leader of the Shiite community.

It was worth noting here that the title "Sayyid", master for the Shi'a, is given to those who are the descendants of the family of the Prophet (saw), and the "Sayyid", whether he is a student or an Alim (learned man), wears a black turban, but other Ulama usually wear white turbans and bear the title of "Shaykh". There are other notables (al-Ashraf) who are not Ulama and wear a green turban.

My friend asked them if I could sit with them, whilst he went to meet al- Sayyid. They welcomed me and sat around me in a semi-circle and I looked at their faces which were full of innocence and purity, and then I remembered the saying of the Prophet (saw) "Man is born to live by nature, so his parents could make him a Jew or a Christian or a Magus" and I said to myself, "Or make him a Shi'i."

They asked me, which country I came from, I answered. "From Tunisia." They asked, "Have you got religious schools?" I answered, "We have universities and schools." I was bombarded by questions from all sides, and all the questions were sharp and concentrated. What could I say to those innocent boys who thought that the Islamic world was full of religious schools where they teach Jurisprudence, Islamic Law, principle of Islam and Qur'anic commentary?

They did not know that in the modern world of Islam we have changed the Qur'anic schools to kindergartens supervised by Christian nuns so should I tell them that they are considered by us as being "backward"? One of the boys asked me, "Which Madhhab (religious school) is followed in Tunis'?" I said, "The Maliki madhhab." And noticed that some of them laughed, but I did not pay much attention. He asked me, "Do you not know the Jafari Madhhab?" I said, "What is this new name? No we only know the four Madhahibs, and apart from that is not within Islam."

He smiled and said, "The Jafari Madhhab is the essence of Islam, do you not know that Imam Abu Hanifah studied under Imam Jafar al-Sadiq? And that Abu Hanifah said, "Without the two years al-Numan would have perished." I remained silent and did not answer, for I had heard a name that I had never heard before, but thanked Allah that he i.e. their Imam Jafar al- Sadiq was not a teacher of Imam Malik, and said that we are Malikis and not Hanafis.

He said, "The four Madhahibs took from each other, Ahmed ibn Hanbal took from al-Shafii, and al-Shafii took from Malik, and Malik took from

Abu Hanifah, and Abu Hanifah from Jafar al-Sadiq, therefore, all of them were students of Jafar ibn Muhammad, who was the first to open an Islamic University in the mosque of his grandfather, the Messenger of Allah and under him studied no less than four thousand jurisprudents and specialists in Hadith (prophetic traditions).

I was surprised by the intelligence of that young boy who seemed to have learnt what he was saying in the same way that one recites a Surah from the Qur'an. I was even more astonished when he started telling me some historical references which he knew the number of their volumes and chapters, and he continued with his discussion as if he was a teacher teaching a student.

In fact I felt weak before him and wished that I had gone with my friend instead of staying with the young boys. I was not able to answer every question connected with jurisprudence or history that they asked me.

He asked me, "Which of the Imams I followed?" I said, "Imam Malik." He said, "How do you follow a dead man with fourteen centuries between you and him. If you want to ask him a question about current issues, would he answer you?" I thought for a little while and then said, "Your Jafar also died fourteen centuries ago, so whom do you follow?" He and other boys answered me quickly, "We follow al- Sayyid al-Khu'i, for he is our Imam."

I did not know who was more knowledgeable, al-Khu'i or Jafar al-Sadiq. I tried my best to change the subject so I kept asking them questions such as, "What is the population of al- Najaf? How far is al-Najaf from Baghdad? Did they know other countries beside Iraq?"

And every time they answered, I prepared another question for them to prevent them from asking me, for I felt incapable of matching their knowledge. But I refused to admit it, despite the fact that inside myself, I accepted defeat. The days of glory and scholarship in Egypt had dissipated here, especially after meeting those youngsters, and then I remembered the following wise words:

Say to him who claims knowledge in Philosophy, "You have known one thing but you are still unaware of many things."

I thought the minds of those young boys were greater than the minds of those Shaykhs whom I met in al-Azhar and the minds of our Shaykhs in Tunisia.

Al-Sayyid al-Khu'i entered the place, and with him came a group of Ulama who looked respectable and dignified, and all the boys stood up, and me with them, then each one of them approached al-Sayyid to kiss his hand, but I stayed rigid in my place. Al-Sayyid did not sit down until everybody sat down, then he started greeting them one by one, and he was greeted back by each individual until my turn came, so I replied in the same way.

After that my friend, who had whispered to al-Sayyid, pointed to me to get nearer to al-Sayyid, which I did, and he sat me to his right. After we exchanged the greetings my friend said to me, "Tell al-Sayyid the things you hear in Tunisia about the Shi'a." I said, "Brother, let us forget about the stories we hear from here and there, and I want to know for myself what the Shi'a say, so I want frank answers to some questions that I have."

My friend insisted that I should inform al-Sayyid about what we thought of al-Shi'a. I said, "We consider the Shi'a to be harder on Islam than the Christian and Jews, because they worship Allah and believe in the Message of Musa, may Allah grant him peace, but we hear that the Shi'a worship 'Ali and consider him to be sacred, and there is a sect among them who worship Allah but put 'Ali at the same level as the Messenger of Allah." Also I told him the story about how the angel Gabriel betrayed his charge, as they say, so instead of giving the message to 'Ali he gave it to Muhammad (saw).

Al-Sayyid remained silent for a little while, with his head down, then he looked at me and said, "We believe that there is no other God but Allah, and that Muhammad (saw) is the Messenger of Allah, and that 'Ali was but a servant of Allah." He turned to his audience and said, indicating to me "Look at these innocent people how they have been brain-washed by the false rumors; and this is not surprising for I heard more than that from other people, (so we say) there is no power or strength save in Allah, the Highest and the Greatest."

Then he turned to me and said, "Have you read the Qur'an?" I answered, "I could recite half of it by heart before I was ten." He said, "Do you know that all the Islamic groups, regardless of their sects agree on the Holy Qur'an, for our Qur'an is the same as yours?" I said, "Yes I know that." He then said, "Have you not read the words of Allah, praise be to Him the Sublime:

> *"And Muhammad is no more than a messenger, the messengers have already passed away before him." (Holy Qur'an 3:144)*

> *"Muhammad is the Messenger of Allah, and those with him are from of heart against the unbelievers." (Holy Qur'an 48:29)*

> *"Muhammad is not the father of any of your men, but he is the Messenger of Allah and the last of the Prophets." (Holy Qur'an 33:40)*

I said, "Yes I know all these Qur'anic verses." He said, "Where is 'Ali then? If our Qur'an says that Muhammad (saw) is the Messenger of Allah, so where did this lie come from?"

I remained silent and could not find an answer. He added, "As for the betrayal of Gabriel, God forbid, it is worse than the first, because when

Allah sent Gabriel unto Muhammad (saw), Muhammad (saw) was forty years old then, and 'Ali was a lad of six or seven years, so how could Gabriel make a mistake and did not differentiate between Muhammad (saw) the man and 'Ali the lad?" He stayed silent for a long time, and I started thinking about what he had said, which appeared to me as logical reasoning, so that it left a deep impression on me, and I asked myself why we did not base our analysis on such logical reasoning.

Al-Sayyid al-Khu'i added, "I would like to inform you that the Shi'a is the only group, among all the Islamic groups, which believe in the infallibility of the Prophets and Imams; so if our Imams, may Allah grant them peace, are infallible, and they are human beings like us, then how about Gabriel, who is an angel favored by Allah and He called him "The faithful spirit"?

I asked, "Where did all these rumors come from?" He said, "From the enemies of Islam who want to divide the Muslims into groups that fight each other, otherwise Muslims are brothers, whether they were Shi'a or Sunnis, for all of them worship Allah alone and do not associate any other God with Him, and they have one Qur'an, one Prophet and one Qiblah (Direction to which Muslims turn in praying i.e. Kabaa). The Shi'a and the Sunnis only differ on issues regarding jurisprudence, in the same way that the different schools of jurisprudence in the Sunni school differ among each other; as Malik did not agree all the way with Abu Hanifah who himself did not agree all the way with al-Shafii and so on."

I said, "Therefore, all the things which have been said about you are just lies?" He said, "You, praise be to Allah, are a sensible man and could comprehend things, also you have seen Shi'i countries and have travelled in their midst; so did you hear or see anything related to these lies?" I said, "No, I have not seen or heard anything but good things, and I thank Allah for giving me the opportunity to meet Mr. Munim on the ship, since he was the reason for my presence in Iraq, and indeed I have learnt many things that I had not known before."

My friend Munim said, with a smile, "Including the existence of a grave for the Imam 'Ali?" I winked at him and said, "In fact I have learnt many new things even from those young lads and wish I had had the opportunity to learn as they do in this Religious School."

Al-Sayyid said, "Welcome, if you want to study here, then there will be a place for you in this school." Everybody welcomed the suggestion, especially my friend Munim whose face was full of joy.

I said, "I am a married man with two boys." He said, "We will take care of your accommodation and living and whatever you need, but the important thing is learning."

I thought for a little while and said to myself, "It does not seem acceptable to become a student after having spent five years as a teacher and educationalist, and it is not easy to take a decision so hastily."

I thanked al-Sayyid al-Khu'i for his offer and told him that I would think about the matter seriously after I came back from al-Umrah, but I needed some books. Al-Sayyid said, "Give him the books."

A group of learned people stood up and went to their book cabinets and after a few minutes each one of them presented me with a book, so I had more than seventy. I realized that I could not carry all these books with me, especially as I was going to Saudi Arabia, where the authorities censor any book entering their countries, lest new ideas get established, in particular those ideas which do not agree with their creed.

However, I did not want to miss the chance of having all these books which I had never seen in all my life. I said to my friend and the rest of the people that I had a long journey ahead of me, passing through Damascus, Jordan and Saudi Arabia, and on the way back my journey would be even longer for I would travel through Egypt and Lybia until I reached Tunisia, and beside the weight of these books was the fact that most of the countries prohibit the entry of these books to their territories.

Al-Sayyid said, "Leave us your address and we will send them to you." I liked the idea and gave him my personal card with my address in Tunis on it. Also, I thanked him for his generosity, and when I was about to leave him he stood up and said to me, "May Allah grant you safety and if you stand by the grave of my forefather the Messenger of Allah please pass my greetings to him."

Everybody, including myself, was moved by what al- Sayyid had said, and I noticed that tears were coming from his eyes, and then I said to myself, "God forbid that such a man could be wrong or a liar; his dignity, his greatness and his modesty tell you that he is truly a descendant of the Prophet." I could not help myself but to take his hand and kiss it, in spite of his refusal.

When I stood up to go, everybody stood and said farewell to me, and some of the young lads from the religious school followed me and asked me for my addresses for future correspondence, and I gave it to them.

We went back to al-Kufa after an invitation from a friend of Munim, whose name was Abu Shubbar, and stayed in his house where we spent a whole night socializing with a group of intellectual young people. Among those people were some students of al-Sayyid Muhammad Baqir al-Sadr who suggested that I should meet him, and they promised to arrange an interview with him on the day after. My friend Munim liked the idea but apologized for not being able to be present at the meeting because he has a prior engagement in Baghdad. We agreed that I would stay in Abu Shubbar's house for three or four days until Munim came back.

Munim left us shortly after the dawn prayers and we went to sleep. I benefitted so much from these students and was surprised about the variety of subjects they study in the Religious School. In addition to the Islamic studies which include Jurisprudence, Islamic Law (Shariah) and Tawheed (Islamic Theology); they study Economics, Sociology, Politics, and History, Languages, Astronomy and a few more subjects.

A Meeting with Al Sayyid Muhammad Baqir al Sadr

I went with Abu Shubbar to al-Sayyid Muhammad Baqir al-Sadr's house, and on the way he honoured me and talked to me about the famous Ulama and about Taqlid (adoption of a legal decision by the Mujtahid) and so on until we entered the house where we found al Sayyid al Sadr surrounded by many young turbaned students.

Al-Sayyid stood up and greeted us, then I was introduced to him and he welcomed me warmly and sat me next to him. After that he started asking me about Tunisia and Algeria and about famous Ulama like al-Khidr Husayn and al-Thahir ibn Ashoor and others. I enjoyed his talk, and despite his high position and the great respect he commands from his students, I found myself at ease with him and felt as if I had known him before.

I benefitted so much from that meeting because I listened to the questions asked by the students and his answers to them; also I appreciated then the idea of adopting the decision of the living Ulama who could answer all sorts of questions directly and clearly. I became convinced that the Shi'a are Muslims worshipping Allah alone, who believe in the message of our Prophet Muhammad (saw).

At the beginning I suspected that what I saw was just acting, or perhaps as they call it Taqiyyah, i.e. they show what they do not believe; but these suspicions disappeared quickly since it was inconceivable that the hundreds of people that I saw or heard coordinated their acting, and why should there be acting anyway?

Besides who was I, and why should they be concerned about me to the extent that they used Taqiyyah with me? And all their books, whether they were old ones that had been written centuries ago or the newly published ones, all professed the unity of Allah and praise His Messenger Muhammad (saw). There I was, in the house of al-Sayyid Muhammad Baqir al-Sadr, the famous religious authority inside Iraq and outside it, and every time the name of Muhammad (saw) was mentioned, the entire audience shouted in one voice "May Allah's blessings be upon Muhammad and his household."

When the time for prayer was due, we left the house and went to the mosque, which was next door, and al-Sayyid Muhammad al-Sadr led the midday and afternoon prayers. I felt as if I was living among the Companions (of the Prophet), for there was a solemn invocation from one of the men who had a moving voice, and when he finished the invocation the whole audience shouted, "May Allah's blessing be upon Muhammad and his household." The invocation was basically to thank and glorify Allah, the Great Majesty, and then Muhammad (saw) and his good and purified posterity.

After the prayer, al-Sayyid sat in the Mihrab (the prayer niche) and people came to greet him, some asked him private questions, others asked him general questions, and he answered each one of them accordingly. When the person obtained an answer for his question, he kissed the hand of al- Sayyid then left, what lucky people to have such a dignified learned Imam who lives their experiences and solves their problems.

Al-Sayyid showed me so much care and generosity to the extent that

I forgot all about my family and tribe, and felt that if I stayed for one month with him, I would have become a Shi'i, because of his manners, modesty and generosity. Whenever I looked at him he smiled and asked me if I needed anything, and I did not leave his company during the four days, only when I wanted to go to sleep.

There were many visitors who came to see him from all over the world; there were Saudi Shi'i from Hijaz, others came from Bahrain, Qatar, United Arab Emirates, Lebanon, Syria, Iran, Afghanistan, Turkey and Black Africa; and al-Sayyid spoke to each one of them and solved their problems, later they left him feeling happy and comforted.

Here I would like to mention a case which was brought to al-Sayyid when I was in his company, and I was very impressed by the way he dealt with it. I mention it because of its historical importance so that the Muslims know what they have lost by leaving the rule of Allah.

Four men, who were probably Iraqis, judging by their accents, came to see al-Sayyid Muhammad Baqir al-Sadr. One of them had inherited a house from his grandfather, who had died a few years ago, and had sold that house to a second person (he was present then). One year after the completion of the sale, two brothers came and proved that they were also legal inheritors of the dead man (i.e. the father).

The four of them sat before al-Sayyid and each one of them produced a number of papers and deeds, which al-Sayyid read, and after he spoke for a few minutes with the men, he passed a fair judgment. He gave the purchaser the full right to his house, and asked the seller to pay to his two brothers their shares from the selling price, and after that they stood up and kissed al-Sayyid's hand and embraced each other. I was astonished about what had happened and asked Abu Shubbar, "Has the case ended?"

He said, "Yes, everyone received his right. Praise be to Allah!" In such case, and in such a short time, only a few minutes, the problem was solved. A similar case in our country would have taken at least ten years to resolve, some of the plaintiffs would die and their sons resume the case; often the legal costs exceed the price of the house. The case would move from the Magistrate Court to the Appeal Court to the Court of Review, and at the end no one is satisfied, and hatred between People and Tribes are created.

Abu Shubbar commented, "we have the same thing if not worse." I asked, "How?" He said, if people take their cases to the state courts, then they would go through the same troubles which you have just mentioned, but if they follow the Religious Authority and commit themselves to the Islamic Laws, then they would take their cases to him and the problem would be solved in a few minutes, as you saw. And what is better than the Law of Allah for people who could comprehend? Al-Sayyid al-Sadr did not charge them one Fils, but if they went to the state courts, then they would have paid a high price."

I said, "Praise be to Allah! I still cannot believe what I have seen, and if I had not seen it with my eyes, I would not have believed it at all."

Abu Shubbar said, "You do not have to deny it brother, this is a simple case in comparison with other more complicated ones which involve blood. Even so, the Religious Authorities do consider them, and it takes them a few hours to resolve." I said with astonishment, "Therefore you have two governments in Iraq, a government of the state and a government of the clergy. He replied, "No, we have a government of the state only, but the Muslims of the Shi'i Madhhab who follow the Religious Authorities, have nothing to do with the government of the state, because it is not an Islamic government.

They are subjects of that government simply because of their citizenship, the taxes, civil laws and personal status; so if a committed Muslim had an argument with a non committed Muslim, then the case must be taken to the state courts, because the latter would not accept the judgment of the Religious Authorities. However, if two committed Muslims had an argument, then there is no problem, whatever the

Religious Authorities decide is acceptable to all parties. Thus, all cases seen by the Religious Authorities are solved on a day-to-day basis, whereas other cases linger on for months and years."

It was an incident that made me feel content with rule of Allah, praise be to Him the Exalted one, which helped me to comprehend the words of Allah in His Glorious Book:

"... And whoever did not judge by what Allah revealed, those are they that are the unbelievers." (Holy Qur'an 5:44)

"... And whoever did not judge by what Allah revealed, those are they that are the unjust." (Holy Qur'an 5:45)

"... And whoever did not judge by what Allah revealed, those are they that are the transgressors." (Holy Qur'an 5:47)

That incident aroused in me feelings of anger and resentment about those who change the just rules of Allah with some unjust, man-made rules. They even go further, and with all impudence and sarcasm, they criticize the divine rules and condemn them for being barbaric and inhuman because it draws the limits cuts the hand of the thief, stones the adulterer and kills the killer. So where did all these new theories that are foreign to us and our culture come from? There is no doubt they came from the West and from the enemies of Islam who know that the application of Allah's rules mean their inevitable destruction because they are thieves, traitors, adulterers, criminals and murderers.

I had many discussions with al-Sayyid al-Sadr during these days, and I asked him about everything I had learnt through the friends who talked to me about their beliefs and what they thought about the Companions of the Prophet (saw), and about 'Ali and his sons, beside many other issues that we used to disagree upon.

I asked al-Sayyid al-Sadr about Imam 'Ali and why they testify for him in the Adhan (the call for prayers) that he is "Waliy Allah" (the friend of Allah). He answered me in the following way:

"The Commander of the Believers, 'Ali, may Allah's blessings be upon him, was one of those servants of Allah whom He chose and honored by giving them the responsibilities of the Message after His Prophet. These servants are the trustees of the Prophet (saw), since each prophet has a trustee, and 'Ali ibn Abi Talib is the trustee of Muhammad (saw).

We favor him above all the Companions of the Prophet (saw) because Allah and the Prophet favored him, and we have many proofs of that, some of them are deduced through logical reasoning, others are found in the Qur'an and al-Sunnah (the Tradition of the Prophet Muhammad (saw)), and these proofs cannot be suspect, because they have been scrutinized, and proven right, by our own learned people (who wrote many books about the subject) and those of the Sunni Madhahibs.

The Umayyad regime worked very hard to cover this truth and fought Imam 'Ali and his sons, whom they killed. They even ordered people, sometimes by force, to curse him, so his followers, may Allah bless them all, started to testify for him as being the friend of Allah. No Muslim would curse the friend of Allah in defiance of the oppressive authorities, so that the glory was to Allah, and to His Messenger and to all the believers. It also became an historical land mark across the generations so that they know the just cause of 'Ali and the wrong doing of his enemies.

Thus, our learned people continued to testify that 'Ali is the friend of Allah in their calls to prayer, as something which is commendable. There are many commendable things in the religious rites as well as in ordinary mundane dealings, and the Muslim will be rewarded for doing them, but not punished for leaving them aside.

For example, it is commendable for the Muslim to say after al-Shahadah (i.e. to testify that there is no God but Allah, and that

Muhammad (saw) is His messenger): And I will testify that Heaven is true and Hell is true, and that Allah will resurrect people from their graves."

I said "Our learned people taught us that the priority of the succession was for our master Abu Bakr al-Siddiq, then to our master Umar al-Faruq, then to our master Uthman, then to our master 'Ali, may Allah bless them all."

Al-Sayyid remained silent for a short while, then answered me: "Let them say what they want, but it would be impossible for them to prove it on legal grounds, besides, what they say contradicts their books which state: The best of the people is Abu Bakr then Uthman, and there is no mention of 'Ali because they made him just an ordinary person, however, the later historians started to mention him for the sake of mentioning the Rightly Guided Caliphs.

After that I asked him about the piece of clay on which they put their foreheads during the prayers and they call it "al-Turbah al-Husayniyyah". He answered,

We all prostrate on the dust, but not for the dust, as some people claim that the Shi'a do, for the prostration is only for Allah, praise be to Him the Highest. It is well established among our people, as well as among the Sunnis, that the most favourable prostration is on earth or on the non-edible produce of the earth, and it is incorrect to prostrate on anything else. The Messenger of Allah (saw) used to sit on the dust, and he had a piece of clay mixed with straw, on which he used to prostrate. He also taught his Companions, may Allah bless them all, to prostrate on the earth or on stones, and forbade them from prostrating on the edges of their shirts. We consider these acts to be necessary and important.

Imam Zayn al-Abideen 'Ali ibn al-Husayn (may Allah bless them both) took a Turbah (a piece of clay) from near the grave of his father Abu

Abdullah, because the dust there is blessed and pure, for the blood of the chief martyr was spilt on it. Thus, his followers continue with that practice up to the present day.

We do not say that prostration is not allowed but on Turbah, rather, we say that prostration is correct if it is done on any blessed Turbah or stone, also it is correct if it is done on a mat which is made of palm leaves or similar material.

I asked, with reference to our master al-Husayn, may Allah's blessings be upon him, "Why do the Shi'a cry and beat their cheeks and other parts of their bodies until blood is spilt, and this is prohibited in Islam, for the Prophet (saw) said: He who beats the cheeks, tears the pockets and follows the call of al-Jahiliyyah is not one of us."

Al-Sayyid replied,

The saying is correct and there is no doubt about it, but it does not apply to the obsequies of Abu Abdullah, for he who calls for the avenging of al- Husayn and follows his path, his call is not of the Jahiliyyah. Besides, the Shias are only human beings, among them you find the learned and not so learned, and they have feelings and emotions. If they are overcome by their emotions during the anniversary of the martyrdom of Abu Abdullah, and remember what happened to him, his family and his companions from degradation to captivity and then finally murder, then they will be rewarded for their good intentions, because all these intentions are for the sake of Allah. Allah - praise be to Him, the Highest - who rewards people according to their intentions.

Last week I read the official reports from the Egyptian government about the suicide incidents that followed the death of Jamal Abdul Nasser. There were eight such incidents in which people took their lives by jumping from buildings or throwing themselves under trains, besides them there were many injured people. These are but some examples in which emotions have overcome the most rational of people, who happen to be Muslims and who killed themselves because of the death of Jamal Abdul Nasser, who died of natural causes, therefore, it is not right for us to condemn the Sunnis and judge them to be wrong.

On the other hand, it is not right for the Sunnis to accuse their brothers the Shi'a of being wrong because they cry for the chief martyr. These people have lived and are still living to this present day the tragedy of al-Husayn. Even the Messenger of Allah (saw) cried after the death of his son al- Husayn, and Gabriel cried also.

I asked, "Why do the Shi'a decorate the graves of their saints with gold and silver, despite the fact that it is prohibited in Islam?"

Al-Sayyid al-Sadr replied,

This is not done just by the Shi'a, and it is not prohibited. Look at the mosques of our brothers the Sunnis in Iraq or Egypt or Turkey or anywhere else in the Islamic world, they are all decorated with gold and silver. Furthermore, the mosque of the Messenger of Allah (saw) in al-Madinah al- Munawarah and the Kaba, the House of Allah, in the blessed Mecca is covered every year by a cloth decorated by gold which costs millions. So such a thing is not exclusive to the Shi'a.

I asked "The Saudi Ulama say that touching the graves and calling the saints for their blessings is polytheism, so what is your opinion?"

Al-Sayyid al-Sadr replied:

If touching the graves and calling the dead is with the understanding that they could cause harm or render a benefit, then that is polytheism, no doubt about it, the Muslims are monotheists and they know that Allah alone could cause harm or render a benefit, but calling the saints and Imams (may Allah bless them all) with the understanding that they could be an intermediary to Allah, that is not polytheism.

All Muslims, Sunnis and Shias, agreed on this point from the time of the Messenger up to the present day, except the Wahabiyyah, the Saudi Ulama who contradict all Muslims with their new creed. They caused considerable disturbances among the Muslims, they accused them of blasphemy, they spilt their blood and even beat old pilgrims on their way to the House of Allah in Mecca just because they say "O Messenger of Allah, may peace be upon you", and they will never let anybody touch his blessed grave. They had so many debates with our learned people, but they persisted in their stubbornness and their arrogance.

Al-Sayyid Sharaf al-Din, a famous Shi'i learned man, went on pilgrimage to the House of Allah during the time of Abdul Aziz ibn Saud, and he was one of those Ulama who were invited to the King's palace to celebrate with the King 'Id al-Adhha, in accordance with the customs there. When his turn came to shake the King's hand, Sayyid Sharaf al-Din presented him with a leather bound Qur'an.

The King took the Qur'an and placed it on his forehead then kissed it. Al Sayyid Sharaf al-Din said, "O King, why do you kiss and glorify the cover which is only made out of goat's skin?" The King answered, "I meant to glorify the Holy Qur'an, not the goat's skin." Al-Sayyid Sharaf al-Din then said, "Well said, O King. We do the same when we kiss the window or the door of the Prophet's (saw) chamber, we know it is made of iron and could not harm or render a benefit, but we mean what is behind the iron and wood, we mean to glorify the Messenger of Allah (saw) in the same way as you meant with the Qur'an when you kissed its goat's skin cover.

The audience was impressed by al-Sayyid and said, "You are right." The King was forced to allow the pilgrims to ask for blessings from the Prophet's relics, until the order was reversed by the successor of that king. The issue is not that they are afraid of people associating others with Allah, rather, it is a political issue based on antagonizing and killing the Muslims in order to consolidate their power and authority over the Muslims, and history is the witness to what they have done with the Muslim nation.

I asked him about the Sufi orders, and he answered me briefly:

There are positive and negative aspects to them. The positive aspects include self-discipline, austere living, renunciation of worldly pleasures and elevating one's self to the spiritual world. The negative aspects include isolation, escapism and restricting the mention of Allah by verbal numbers and various other practices. Islam, as it is known accepts the positive aspects but rejects the negative ones, and we may say that all the principles and teachings of Islam are positive.

Skepticism and Perplexity

The answers of al-Sayyid al-Sadr were clear and convincing, but it was very difficult for a person like me to comprehend them. Twenty-five years of my life had been based on the idea of glorifying and respecting the Companions of the Prophet, especially the Rightly Guided Caliphs. The Messenger of Allah commanded us to follow their teachings, in particular Abu Bakr al-Siddiq and Umar al-Farooq, but I had never heard their names mentioned since I arrived in Iraq. Instead, I heard strange names that I had never come across before, and that there were twelve Imams, and a claim that the Messenger of Allah had stated before his death that Imam 'Ali should be his successor.

How could I believe all that (that all Muslims and the Companions of the Prophet- who was the best of people -, after the death of the Prophet agreed to stand against 'Ali - may Allah honor him) when we had been taught from childhood that the Companions of the Prophet - may Allah bless them all - respected 'Ali and knew very well what kind of man he was. They knew that he was the husband of Fatima al-Zahra and the father of al-Hasan and al-Husayn and the gate to the city of knowledge.

Skepticism and Perplexity

Our Master 'Ali knew the quality of Abu Bakr al-Siddiq, who became a Muslim before anybody else, and accompanied the Prophet to the cave, as is mentioned by Allah, the Mighty, in the Qur'an, and whom the Messenger of Allah charged with the leadership of the prayers during his illness, and said about him, if I was taking a very close friend, I would have chosen Abu Bakr." Because of all that, the Muslims elected him as their caliph.

Imam 'Ali knew the position of our master Umar, with whom Allah glorified Islam, and the Messenger of Allah called him al-Farooq, he who separates right from wrong. Also Imam 'Ali knew the position of our master Uthman, in whose presence the angels of the Merciful felt shy, and who organized al-Usrah's army, and who was named by the Messenger of Allah as "Dhu al-Nurayn", the man who is endowed with two lights.

How could our brothers, al-Shi'a, ignore or pretend to ignore all that, and make these personalities just ordinary characters subject to all worldly whims and greed so that they deviated from the right path and disobeyed the orders of the Messenger after his death. This was inconceivable since we know that these people used to hasten to execute the orders of the Messenger; they killed their sons and fathers and members of their tribes for the sake of glorifying Islam and its ultimate victory. He who would kill his father and son for the sake of Allah and His Messenger could not be subject to worldly and transitory ambitions such as the position of Caliph, and ignoring the orders of the Messenger of Allah.

Yes, because of all that I could not believe all the Shi'a were saying, in spite of the fact that I was convinced about many things. I remained in a state of doubt and perplexity: doubtful because of what the Shii learned scholars Ulama said to me, which I found sensible and logical; and perplexed because I could not believe that the Companions of the Prophet, may Allah bless them all, would sink to such a low moral stand and become ordinary people like us, neither sharpened by the light of the Message nor able to be enlightened by Muhammad.

O my God, how could that be? Could the Companions of the Prophet be at the level described by the Shi'a? The important thing is that doubt and perplexity were the beginning of weakness and the realization that there were many hidden issues to be uncovered before reaching the truth.

My friend came, then we travelled to Karbala, and there I lived the tragedy of our master al-Husayn in the same way his followers, and only then did I know that he had not died an ordinary death. People tend to crowd around his grave like butterflies and cry with such sorrow and grief that I have never seen before, as if al-Husayn had just been martyred. I heard speakers who aroused the feelings of people when describing the incident at Karbala, accompanied by crying and wailing, and soon the listener loses control of himself and collapses.

I cried and cried and let myself go as if crushed, and felt a relief that I had never experienced before that day; I felt that I had been in the ranks of al-Husayn's enemies and had suddenly changed sides to be one of his followers who sacrificed themselves for his sake. The speaker was reciting the story of al-Hurr, who was one of the commanders in charge of fighting al-Husayn, who stood in the middle of the battlefield shaking like a leaf, and when one of his friends asked him, "Are you afraid of death?" He answered, "No, by Allah, but I am choosing between heaven and hell." Then he kicked his horse and went towards al-Husayn and asked, "Is there a repentance, O son of the Messenger of Allah?"

When I heard that, I could not control myself and fell on the floor crying and felt as if I was in the position of al-Hurr, asking al-Husayn, "Is there repentance, O son of the Messenger of Allah? Forgive me O son of the Messenger of Allah. The voice of the speaker was so moving that people started crying and wailing, and when my friend heard my cries, he embraced me, like a mother embracing her child, and started crying and calling, "O Husayn...O Husayn..."

These were moments, during which I learnt that meaning of real crying and felt that my tears washed my heart and body from the inside, and then I understood the meaning of the Messenger's saying: If you knew what I know, you would have laughed little and cried more.

I was depressed throughout the day, although my friend tried to re-assure me and cheer me up by offering me some refreshments, but I had lost my appetite completely. I asked him to repeat the story of the martyrdom of al- Husayn, for I did not know much about it except the fact that our religious leaders told us that the enemies of Islam killed our masters Umar, Uthman and 'Ali, and that the same enemies killed our master al-Husayn; and that is all we knew. In fact we used to celebrate Ashura, as one of the festival days of Islam; alms were distributed and various types of food were cooked and the young boys went to their elders who gave them money to buy sweets and toys.

However, there are a few customs in some villages during Ashura: people do not light fires or do any kind of work. People do not get married or celebrate a happy occasion. We usually accept them at face value without any explanation given, and strangely enough, our religious leaders talk to us about the greatness of Ashura and how blessed it is.

After that we went to visit the grave of al-Abbas, the brother of al-Husayn. I did not know who he was, but my friend informed me about his bravery. We also met many pious religious leaders whose names I cannot recall in detail, but I can still recall their surnames: Bahr al-Ulum, al-Sayyid al-Hakim, Kashif al-Ghita, al-Yasin, al-Tabatabai, al-Feiruzabadi, Asad Haidar, and others, who honoured me with their company.

They are truly pious religious leaders, possessing all the signs of dignity and respect, and the Shi'a population respects them and gives them one fifth of their incomes.

Through these donations they manage the affairs of the religious schools, open new schools, establish presses and assist students who come to them from all over the Islamic world.

They are independent and not connected in any way with the rulers; unlike our religious leaders who would not do or say anything without the approval of the authorities, who pay their salaries and appoint them, and remove them whenever they want.

It was a new world that I had discovered, or rather, Allah had discovered for me. I started to enjoy it having previously kept away from it, and gradually blended with it after I had opposed it. I gained new ideas from this new world, and it inspired me with the quest for knowledge and research until I reached the desired truth which always comes to mind whenever I read the saying of the prophet:

The sons of Israel were divided into seventy-one groups, and the Christians were divided into seventy-two groups, and my people will be divided into seventy-three groups, all of which, except one group will end up in Hell.

Here is not the place to talk about the various religions which claim to be the right one and that the rest are wrong, but I am surprised and astonished whenever I read this saying. My surprise and astonishment is not at the saying itself, but at those Muslims who read it and repeat it in their speeches and brush over it without analyzing it or even attempting to find out which the group is going to be saved and which are going to be doomed.

The interesting thing is that each group claims that it is the saved one. At the end of the saying came the following: "Who are they, O Messenger of Allah?" He answered, "Those who follow my path and the path of my Companions." Is there any group that does not adhere to the Book (Qur'an) and Sunnah (the prophetic tradition), and is there any Islamic group that claims otherwise? If Imams Malik or Abu Hanifah or al-Shafii or Ahmed ibn Hanbel were asked, wouldn't each and every one of them claim that he adheres to the teachings of the Qur'an and the Right Sunnah'?

These are the Sunni Madhahib, in addition to the various Shi'i-groups, which I had believed at one time to be deviant and corrupt. All of them claim to adhere to the Qur'an and the correct Sunnah which has been handed down through Ahl al-Bayt (the Prophets Family) who knew best about what they were saying. Is it possible that they are all right, as they claim?

This is not possible, because the Prophets saying states the opposite, unless the saying is invented or fabricated. But that is not possible either, because the saying is accepted by both the Shi'a and Sunnis. Is it possible that the saying has no meaning? God forbid that His Messenger (saw) could utter a meaningless and aimless saying, as he only spoke words of wisdom. Therefore we are left with one possible conclusion: that there is one group which is on the right path and that the rest are wrong. Thus, the saying tends to make one confused and perplexed, but in the meantime it encourages research and study by those who want to be saved.

Because of that, I became doubtful and perplexed after my meeting with the Shi'a, for who knows, they might be saying the truth! So should I not study and investigate?

Islam, through the Qur'an and Sunnah ordered me to study, investigate and to compare, and Allah, the Most High said:

"And (as for) those who strive hard for Us, We will most certainly guide them in Our ways." (Holy Qur'an 29:69)

He also said: "Those who listen to the word then follow the best of it; these are they whom Allah has guided, and those it is who are the men of understanding." (Holy Qur'an 39:18)

The Messenger of Allah (saw) said: "Study your religion until it is said that you are mad."

Therefore research and comparison are legal obligations for every responsible person.

Having reached this decision and resolution, and with this promise to myself and my Shi'i friends from Iraq, I embraced them and bade them farewell, full of sorrow since I liked them and they liked me. I felt that I had left dear and faithful friends who had sacrificed their time in order to help me. They did it out of their own choice and asked for nothing except the approval of Allah, Praise be to Him. The Prophet (saw) said, "If Allah chooses you to guide one man (to the right path), then that is worth more than all the riches on earth."

I left Iraq having spent twenty days among the Imams and their followers, and the time had passed like a nice dream from which the sleeper was loathe to awake. I left Iraq feeling sorry for the brevity of this period and sorry to leave dear friends who were full of love for Ahl-al-Bayt.

I left Iraq for the Hijaz seeking the House of Allah and the grave of the Master of the First and the Last (saw).

The Journey to Hijaz

I arrived in Jeddah and met my friend al-Basheer, who was very pleased to see me and took me to his home and showed me the highest degree of generosity. We spent the time by going around in his car visiting places, and did the Umrah together, and we spent a few days together full of worshipping and other pious works. I apologized to my friend for being late due to my long stay in Iraq and told him about my new discovery, or rather new faith.

He was open minded and well informed, so he said to me, "This is true, for I hear that they have some great learned scholars, but also they have many deviant groups that cause us considerable trouble during the pilgrimage. I asked him, "What are these problems they cause?" He said, "They pray around the graves and enter al-Baqee in groups crying and wailing and they carry with them pieces of stones on which they prostrate themselves; and if they visit the grave of our master al-Hamzah in Uhud, they make up a funeral ceremony, beating their chests and wailing as if al- Hamza had just died. Because of all that, the Saudi government prevented them from visiting the graves."

I laughed and said, "Is it because of that you judge them as being deviant from Islam?" He said, "That and other reasons. They come to visit the Prophets (saw) grave, but at the same time they stand around the graves of Abu Bakr and Umar and curse them, and some of them throw dirt and litter on the graves."

When I heard these allegations I remembered what my father had told me when he came back from the Pilgrimage that they throw dirt on the Prophet's (saw) grave. There is no doubt that my father never saw them with his own eyes because he said, "We noticed some soldiers from the Saudi Army beating a few pilgrims with sticks and when we protested against their humiliating treatment of the pilgrims of the House of Allah, they answered us: These are not Muslims, they are Shi'a who brought dirt to throw on the Prophet's (saw) grave. My father said: We then left them at that, and cursed them and spat at them."

And now I heard from my Saudi friend who was born in al-Medinah al- Munawwarah that they came to visit the Prophet's (saw) grave but throw dirt on Abu Bakr's and Umar's graves. I became suspicious of the two stories, for I had been on pilgrimage and had seen the blessed room where the graves of Prophet (saw) and Abu Bakr and Umar are locked and nobody could come near them to touch the door or window or indeed to throw anything inside them for two reasons.

Firstly there are no gaps, and secondly there is a strict guard with tough soldiers watching each door, and every one of them carries a whip in his hand to beat the pilgrims who dare to enter the room. It is very likely that some of the Saudi soldiers in their prejudice against the Shi'a accused them with these allegations to justify their aggression towards them or perhaps to provoke other Muslims to fight them and to spread rumors in their countries, that the Shi'a hate the Messenger of Allah and throw dirt on his grave, thus killing two birds with one stone.

A distinguished man whom I trusted told me the following story: We were going around the House of Allah when suddenly a young man suffered a severe pain in his stomach and vomited. The soldiers who were guarding the Black Stone started beating the man and accused him of defiling al- Kaba. He was taken out in a deplorable way then was tried and executed the same day.

All these dramatic stories went round in my mind and I thought for a second about the justification of my Saudi friend for blaspheming the Shi'a, but could not find anything apart from the fact that they beat their chests and cry and prostrate themselves on stones, besides the fact that they pray by the graves. I asked myself, "Is this sufficient proof to blaspheme he who believes that there is no God but Allah and that Muhammad (saw) is His Servant and His Messenger? And he prays, gives alms, fasts Ramadan, visits the House of Allah on pilgrimage, does good deeds and prevents bad deeds.

I did not want to antagonize my friend and to enter into a useless discussion with him so I briefly said, "May Allah enlighten us and enlighten them, and lead us on the right path, and may Allah curse the enemies of Islam and the Muslims."

Every time I went around the House of Allah during al-Umrah, and during my visit to the Blessed Mecca where I found only a few visitors, I prayed and asked Allah genuinely to open my eyes and to lead me to the truth. I stood by the place of Ibrahim (a.s.) and recited the following verse from the Qur'an:

> *"And strive hard in (the way of) Allah (such) a striving as is due to Him: He has chosen you and has not laid upon any hardship in religion; the faith of your father Ibrahim; he named you Muslims before and in this, that the Messenger may be a bearer of witness to you, and you may be bearers of witness to the people; therefore keep up prayer and pay the alms and hold fast by Allah, He is your Guardian, how excellent the Guardian and how excellent the Helper." (Holy*

Qur'an 22:78)

Then I started calling our master Ibrahim or rather our forefather Ibrahim, as the Qur'an calls him: "O Father, you, who called us Muslims. your off spring have disagreed after you, some of them became Jews, others Christians and some others became Muslims; and the Jews were divided among themselves into seventy one groups the Christians were divided into seventy two groups and the Muslims were divided into seventy-three groups; all of them are in darkness, as you told your son Muhammad (saw) but only one group stayed faithful to your oath. O Father!

Is it the way that Allah wants it to be for His creation, as the fatalists believe, so Allah assigns to each soul its destiny, to be Jewish or Christian or Muslim or atheist or polytheist; or is it for the love of this world and deviation from Allah's commands, that they forget Allah, so that He makes them forget themselves."

I could not make myself believe in fatalism, and that Allah assigns a destiny to each individual, rather I tend to believe that Allah has created us and inspired us to understand what is right and what is wrong, and sent us His messengers to explain the complicated matters and to show us what is right or wrong. But man fell under the spell of this life's temptation and with all his arrogance, selfishness, ignorance, curiosity, stubbornness, injustice and tyranny deviated from the right path and followed the devil.

He distanced himself from the Merciful, so he lost his way, and the Holy Qur'an expressed that in the best way in the words of Allah:

"Surely Allah does not do any injustice to men, but men are unjust to themselves." (Holy Qur'an 10:44)

O our father Ibrahim! We cannot blame the Jews nor the Christians for not following the right path after they have been shown the way. Look at this nation which Allah rescued when He sent your son Muhammad (saw) to it, who took it out of the darkness and enlightened it and made it the best nation in the world. It too has been divided into too many warring groups, despite the fact that the Messenger of Allah (saw) has warned them and pressed them until he said, "It is forbidden for a Muslim not to speak to his brother Muslim more than three times."

Whatever happened to this nation which is divided into many small and warring states, some of which do not even know one another. O our father Ibrahim, whatever happened to this nation. It used to be the best nation in the world; it ruled from the East to the West and introduced knowledge and enlightenment to other nations.

Today it has reached a low ebb in its history; its land has been violated and its people have been expelled... Its al-Aqsa Mosque is occupied by a Zionist gang and no one is able to liberate it. If one visits their countries, one will find nothing except wretched poverty, terminal hunger, barren lands, diseases, bad manners, intellectual and technical backwardness, tyranny, persecution, and dirt. It is enough to compare the toilets in Western Europe to that in our countries, and see how much difference there is in hygiene between the two.

It is ironic to find this low level of hygiene in our countries despite the fact that Islam has taught us that "cleanliness is a sign of faith, and dirt is a sign of the devil". Has the faith moved to Europe and the devil come to live in our midst? Why Muslims are frightened to declare their faith even in their own countries!

Why the Muslim cannot even be the master of his own face, since he cannot grow his own beard! The Muslims cannot dress in Islamic costumes, whereas the sinful publicly drink alcohol and commit awful wrongs, and the Muslim cannot even correct them and show them the right way. In fact I have been informed that in some Islamic countries like Egypt or Morocco there are fathers who send their daughters to sell their bodies, out of need and poverty, may there be no power or might but that of Allah the High and the Mighty.

O God why have you abandoned this nation and left it in darkness? No, my God, please forgive me, for it is this nation that abandoned You and chose the devil's path, and you, with all Your wisdom and might said, and Your saying is the truth:

"And whoever turns himself away from the remembrance of the Merciful God, We appoint for him a devil, so he becomes his associate." (Holy Qur'an 43:36)

There is no doubt that the deterioration of the Islamic nation to this low state of submissiveness and backwardness is a sign of its deviation from the right path, and a small minority or one group among seventy three would not affect the destiny of a whole nation.

The Messenger of Allah (saw) said: "You are commanded to do good deeds and to prevent any objectionable act; otherwise Allah will put your wicked ones in charge of you, then your good people would call, but no one will listen to them."

O God, we believe in what you have sent us and we follow the Messenger, so will you consider us with the believers? O God, please do not change our hearts after you have enlightened us. Please God, have mercy on us, for you are the Giver. O God, we have unjustly treated ourselves, and if you do not forgive us and have mercy on us, then we will certainly be among the losers.

I left for al-Medinah al-Munawwarah with a letter from my friend al- Basheer for one of his relatives there, so that I could reside with him during my stay in al-Medinah.

He had already spoken to him on the phone, and when I arrived he received me warmly and put me up in his house. As soon as I arrived,

I went to visit the grave of the Messenger of Allah (saw), so I cleaned myself and put on my best clothes.

There were only a few visitors in comparison to those who come during the season of Pilgrimage, therefore I managed to stand before the graves of the Messenger of Allah (saw), Abu Bakr and Umar, something which I could not do during the Pilgrimage because of the crowds. As I tried to touch the doors for blessing, one of the guards rebuked me, and when I stayed for a long time to do my supplication and salutation, the guards ordered me to leave. I tried to speak to one of the guards, but it was in vain. I went back to the blessed court and sat down to read the Qur'an and to improve my recitation of it. I repeated the recitation several times because I felt as if the Messenger of Allah (saw) was listening to me. I said to myself: Is it conceivable that the Messenger (saw) is dead like any other dead person? If so, why do we say in our prayers "May peace be with you O great prophet, and may Allah's mercy and blessings be upon you" in a form which sounds as if we were addressing him. The Muslims believe that our master al-Khidr (sa) is not dead, and that he would return the greetings of anybody who greets him.

Also, the followers of the Sufi orders believe that their Shaykhs, Ahmed al-Tijani or Abdul Qadir al-Jilani come to see them openly and not in their sleep, so why are we reluctant to grant this noble deed to the Messenger of Allah, and he is the best of all mankind? But the reassuring thing is that the Muslims are not reluctant towards the Messenger of Allah except the Wahabis, from whom, for this and various other reasons, I started to feel estranged. I found their manners very coarse, because they treat other Muslims who disagree with their beliefs very harshly. I visited al-Baqee Cemetery once, and while I was calling for mercy upon the souls of Ahl al-Bayt, I noticed an old man standing near me crying, and because of that I realized he was a Shi'i.

He positioned himself towards the Kaba and started to pray, and suddenly a soldier rushed towards him, as if he had been monitoring his moves, and kicked him while he was in a position of prostration. The man fell on his back unconscious, and then the soldier started beating him and cursing him. I felt so sorry for the old man and thought he might have been killed and so I shouted at the soldier, "You must not do that! Why did you beat him while he was praying?" He rebuked me and said, "You be quiet and do not interfere, or else I will do to you what I have just done to him!"

I realized that the soldier was full of aggression, so I avoided him, but I felt angry at myself for not being able to help those who are unjustly treated, and felt angry at the Saudis who treat the people as they like without any check or accountability for their actions. There were some visitors who witnessed the attack, but all that they could do was to say, "There is no power or might but in Allah." Others said, "He deserves what he got because he was praying by the graves."

I could not control myself, so I said to that particular person, "Who told you that we must not pray by the graves? He answered, ' The Messenger of Allah (saw) prevented us from doing so." I replied angrily. You are lying about the Messenger of Allah." I became aware of the dangerous situation and feared that some of the visitors might call the soldier to attack me, so I said gently, if the Messenger of Allah prevented us from praying by the graves, why should millions of pilgrims and visitors disobey him and commit a sin by praying by the graves of the Prophet (saw), Abu Bakr and Umar in the Holy Mosque of the Prophet and in many other mosques around the Islamic world.

Even if praying by the graves is a sin, should it be prevented with such harshness? Or should we prevent it by gentle action. Allow me to tell you the story of the man who urinated in the mosque of the Messenger of Allah and in his presence, and some of his Companions drew their swords to kill him, but he stopped them and said: Let him go and do not harm him, and pour some water on the place where he urinated. We are sent to make things easy and not difficult. We are sent to spread the good words and not to make people keep away from us.

The Companions obeyed his orders, and the Messenger of Allah (saw) asked that man to come and sit next to him and spoke to him nicely. He explained to him that the place was the House of Allah and should not be dirtied, and the man seemed to have understood the point, for he later was seen in the mosque wearing his best and cleanest clothes. Allah - the Great - was right when He said to His Messenger (saw):

"If you had been rough and hard-hearted with them, they would certainly have dispersed from around you." (Holy Qur'an 3:159)

Some of the visitors were moved when they heard the story, and one of them took me aside and asked me, "Where do you come from?" I said, "From Tunisia." He then greeted me and said, "O brother, by Allah, take care of yourself and do not say such things here at all, and this is my advice to you, for the sake of Allah."

I became so angry and bitter about those who claim that they are the guardians of al-Haramayn and treat the guests of the Merciful with such harshness, so that no one is allowed to voice an opinion or to believe in a belief that does not suit their way of thinking, or indeed, to recite a saying (of the Prophet) that does not coincide with their own recitation of the sayings.

I went back to the house of my new friend, whose name I did not then know, and he brought me some supper and sat in front of me and asked me where I had been. I told him my story from the beginning to the end and said, "My brother, I have started to be dissatisfied with the Wahabis and have begun to lean towards the Shi'a."

Suddenly the expression on his face changed and he said to me, "I warn you not to say anything like that again!" Then he left me without even finishing his supper, although I waited for him, until I went to sleep. I woke up next morning with the call for prayers from the Mosque of the Prophet (saw), and found the food was untouched, which meant that my host had never come back.

I became suspicious and feared that the man might have been a member of the secret service, so I left the house quickly and went to the Prophet's Mosque praying and worshipping. After the afternoon prayers I noticed a speaker giving a lesson to some worshippers, so I went towards him, and later learnt from one of the listeners that he was the Qadi (magistrate) of al-Medinah. I listened to him as he was explaining some Qur'anic verses, and after he had finished his lesson and was about to leave, I stopped him and asked him, "Please Sir, could you give me some indications as regard the interpretation of the following Qur'anic verse:

'And Allah only desires to keep away the un-cleanness from you, O people of the House, and to purify you a (thorough) purifying.' (Holy Qur'an 33:33)

I asked, "Who is being referred to as Ahl al-Bayt in this Qur'anic verse?" He answered me immediately, "The wives of the Prophet (saw), and the verse started by mentioning them:

'O wives of the Prophet, you are not like any other women, if you fear God.' (Holy Qur'an 22:32)

I said to him, "The Shi'a Ulama say that it is 'Ali, Fatima, al-Hasan and al-Husayn, but of course I disagree with them because the beginning of the verse states: O wives of the Prophet. But they answered me as follows. That if the verse meant them (i.e. the wives of the Prophet), then the grammatical form would have been feminine throughout. But the Highest says:

"You are not (like any other women) if you fear God, be not soft in your speech, speak, stay in your houses, do not display your finery, keep up your prayers, give the alms, obey Allah and His Messenger." (All the above verbs are in the feminine form.)

And then, in the section of the verse which refers to Ahl al-Bayt, the form changes, so He says: "To keep away the uncleanness ... and to purify you (in the masculine grammatical form)."

He removed his spectacles and looked at me then said, "Beware of these poisonous ideas, the Shias change the words of Allah in the way they like, and they have many verses about 'Ali and his off-spring that we do not

know. In fact they have a special Qur'an. They call it The Qur'an of Fatimah. I warn you not to be deceived by them."

I replied, "Do not worry sir, I am on my guard, and I know many things about them, but I just wanted to find out." He asked, "Where are you from?" I said, "From Tunisia." He asked, "What is your name?" I replied, "Al- Tijani." He laughed with arrogance and said, "Do you know who Ahmed al- Tijani was?" I answered, "He was the Shaykh of a Sufi order."

He said, "He was an agent of the French Colonial authorities, and the French Colonial system established itself in Algeria and Tunisia with his help, and if you visit Paris go to the National Bibliothique and read for yourself in the French Dictionary under "A" and you will find France gave the Legion de Honour to Ahmed al-Tijani who gave them incalculable help."

I was surprised at what he said, but I thanked him and bade him farewell. I stayed in al-Medinah for a whole week, and I prayed forty

prayers and visited all the holy places. During my stay there I made very careful observations, and as a result I became more and more critical of the
Wahabis.

I left al-Medinah al-Munawwarah and went to Jordan to see some friends I had met while on my way to the pilgrimage, as I indicated before. I stayed with them for three days, and found them full of hatred towards the Shi'a, more so than the people in Tunisia.

There were the same stories and the same rumors, and everyone I asked for proof, answered that "he had heard about them," but I found nobody who had had contact with the Shi'a or read a book by the Shi'a or even met a Shi'i in all his life.

From Jordan I went to Syria, and in Damascus I visited the Umayyad Mosque, next to which is the place where the head of our master al-Husayn is resting; also I visited the grave of Salah al-Din al-Ayyubi and our lady Zaynab bint 'Ali ibn Abi Talib.

From Beirut I took a ship that was going directly to Tripoli. The journey lasted for four days, during which I relaxed physically and mentally. I reviewed the whole trip in my mind and concluded that I had developed an inclination and respect towards the Shi'a; in the meantime I started to resent and keep away from the sinister Wahabis. I thanked Allah for what He had given me and for His care and asked Him, Praise he to Him the Highest, to lead me to the right path.

I arrived home eager to meet my family and friends and found them all well. I was surprised when I entered my house and found many books had arrived home before me but I knew where they had come from. When I opened these books, which filled the whole house, I felt grateful to those people who had not broken their promises. In fact the books they sent me by post exceeded the number of books that had been given to me as presents there.

The Beginning of the Research

I was very grateful for the books which I organized and kept in a special place, which called the library. I rested for a few days, and received the time-table for the new academic year, and found out that I had to work for three consecutive days, and that for the rest of the week I was off-duty.

I started reading the books, so I read "The Beliefs of al-Imamiyya" and "The Origin and Principles of al-Shi'a," and felt that my mind was at ease with the beliefs and ideas of the Shi'a. Then I read "al-Murajaat (correspondences)" by al-Sayyid Sharaf al-Din al-Musawi.

As soon as I read the first few pages, I became engrossed in it and could not leave it unless it was necessary, and even took it with me to the institute. I was surprised at the straight forward clarity of the Shi'i scholar when he solved problems that appeared complicated to the Sunni scholar from al- Azhar.

I found my objective in the book, because it is not like any ordinary book where the author writes whatever he likes without criticism or discussion, for "al-Murajaat" is in the form of a dialogue between two scholars, who belong to a different creed, and are critical of each other's statement. Both base their analysis on the two important references for all Muslims: The Holy Qur'an and the Right Sunnah which is approved in Sihah al-Sittah. I found that there was something common between myself and the idea of the book: for I was an investigator searching for the truth, and was willing to accept it wherever it was found. Therefore I found this book immensely useful, and I owe it a great deal.

I was astonished when I found him talking about the refusal of some of the Companions to comply with the orders of the Prophet(saw), and he gave many examples, including the incident of "Raziyat Yawm al-Khamis (The Calamity of Thursday)", for I could not imagine that our master Umar ibn al-Khattab had disagreed with the orders of the Messenger of Allah (saw) and accused him of Hajjr (talking irrationally), and I thought at the beginning that it was just a story from the Shi'a books. However, I was even more astonished when I noticed that the Shi'i scholar made his reference to the incident in the "Sahih of al-Bukhari" and the "Sahih of Muslim".

I travelled to the Capital, and from there I bought the "Sahih of al-Bukhari", the "Sahih of Muslim", and the "Mosnad of Imam Ahmed", the "Sahih of al-Tirmidhi", the "Muwatta of Imam Malik" and other famous books. I could not wait to get back to the house and read these books, so throughout the journey between Tunis and Gafsah I sat in the bus looking through the pages of al-Bukhari's book searching for the incident of "The great misfortune of Thursday" and hoping that I would never find it.

Nevertheless, I found it and read it many times; and there it was, exactly as it has been cited by al-Sayyid Sharaf al-Din.

I tried to deny the incident in its entirety, and could not believe that our master Umar had played such a dangerous role; but how could I deny it since it was mentioned in our Sihahs; the Sihahs of al-Sunnah, in whose contents we are obliged to believe, so if we doubt them or deny some of them, it means that we abandon all our beliefs.

If the Shi'a scholar had referred to their books, I would not have believed what he said, but he was referring to the Sihahs of al-Sunnah, which could not be challenged, because we are committed to believe that they are the most authentic books after the Book of Allah. Therefore, the issue is a compelling one, because if we doubt these Sihahs we are left with hardly any of the rules and regulations of Islam to rely on.

This is because the rules and regulations which are mentioned in the Book of Allah take the form of general concepts rather than details. We are far from the time of the Message, and have thus inherited the rules of our religion through our fathers and grandfathers with the help of these Sihahs, which cannot be ignored.

As I was about to embark on long and difficult research, I promised myself to depend only on the correct Hadiths that are agreed by both the Shi'a and the Sunnah, and that I would drop all the sayings which are mentioned exclusively by one group or the other. Only through this just method could I keep myself safe from emotional factors, sectarian fanaticism and national tendencies. In the meantime I would be able to pass through the road of doubt and reach the mountain of certainty, and that is the correct path of Allah.

The Companions of the Prophet as seen by the Shi'a and the Sunnis

One of the most important studies which I consider to be the cornerstone for all the studies that lead to the truth is the research into the life of the Companions, their affairs, their deeds and their beliefs; because they were the foundations of everything, and from them we took the principles of our religion, and they enlightened our darkness, so that we can see the rules of Allah. Many Muslim scholars- convinced of the above - embarked on the study of the lives and deeds of the Companions, among them: "Usd al-Ghabah fi Tamyeez al-Sahabah", and "al-Isabah fi Maarifat al-Sahabah", and "Mizan al-I'tidal" and various other books which look critically and analytically at the lives of the Companions, but all from the point of view of the Sunnis.

There is a slight problem here, and that is that most of the early scholars wrote in the way which suited the Umayyad and Abbasid rulers who were well known for their opposition to Ahl al-Bayt and all their followers. Therefore, it is not fair to depend on their works alone without reference to the works of the other Muslim scholars who were persecuted and ultimately killed by these governments simply because they were followers of Ahl al- Bayt and the cause behind the revolutions against the oppressive and deviant authorities.

The main problem with all that was the Companions themselves, for they disagreed about the wish of the Messenger of Allah (saw) to write them a document which would help them to remain on the right path until the Day of Judgment. This disagreement deprived the Islamic nation of a unique virtue, and has thrown it into darkness until it was divided and plagued with internal quarrels and finally ended up as a spent force.

It was they who disagreed on the issue of the Caliphate (the successorship of the Prophet), and were divided between a ruling and an opposing party, thus dividing the nation into the followers of 'Ali and the followers of Muawiyah. It was they who differed in the interpretations of the Book of Allah and the sayings of His Messenger, which led to the creation of the various creeds, groups and subgroups; and from them came many scholars of scholastic theology and schools of thoughts and philosophies inspired by political ambitions with one aim in mind and that was to obtain power.

The Muslims would not have been divided and in disagreement had it not been for the Companions, for every disagreement that has been created in the past, or is being created at the present time is due to their disagreement about the Companions. There is one God, one Qur'an, one Messenger and one Qiblah, and they all agree on that, but the disagreement among the Companions started on the first day after the death of the Messenger (saw), in the Saqifah (house) of Bani Saidah, and has continued up to the present day, and will continue for as long as Allah wills it.

Through my discussions with the Shiite scholars, I discovered that, in their views, the Companions were divided into three categories:

The first category included the good Companions who knew Allah and His Messenger truly well, and they acclaimed him (the Messenger) to the last moments of their lives. They were truly his friends by words and deeds, and they never abandoned him, but rather stood their ground with him. Allah - the most High - praised them in many places in His Holy Book, and the Messenger of Allah (saw) also praised them in many places. This group of Companions are mentioned by the Shi'a with reverence and respect, they are also mentioned by the Sunnis with the same reverence and respect.

The second category were the Companions who embraced Islam and followed the Messenger of Allah (saw) either through choice or through fear, and they always showed their gratitude to the Messenger of Allah (saw) for their Islam. However, they hurt the Messenger of Allah (saw) on a few occasions, and did not always follow his orders, in fact they often challenged him and challenged the clear text with their points of view, until Allah, through the Holy Qur'an, had to intervene by rebuking them or threatening them. Allah exposed them in many Qur'anic verses, also the Messenger of Allah (saw) warned them in many of his sayings. The Shi'a mention this group of Companions only because of their deeds, and without respect or reverence.

The third type of Companions were the hypocrites who accompanied the Messenger of Allah (saw) to deceive him. They pretended to be Muslims but inside themselves they were bent on blasphemy and on deceiving Islam and the Muslims as a whole. Allah has revealed a complete Surah in the Qur'an about them, and mentioned them in many other places, and promised them the lowest level in Hell. Also the Messenger of Allah (saw) mentioned them and issued warnings about them, and even informed some of his close friends about their names and characteristics. The Shi'a and the Sunnis agree in cursing this group of Companions and have nothing to do with them.

There was a special group of Companions who distinguished themselves from the others by being relatives of the Prophet (saw), in addition to having possessed ethical and spiritual virtues and personal distinctions from Allah and His Messenger that no one else was honored with. These were Ahl al- Bayt (the Prophet's Family) whom Allah cleansed and purified, and ordered us to pray for them in the same way as he ordered us to pray for His Messenger.

He made it obligatory for us to pay them one fifth of our income, and that every Muslim must love them as a reward for the Muhammadan Message. They are our leaders and we must obey them; and they are people firmly rooted in knowledge who know the interpretation of the Holy Qur'an and they know the decisive verses of it, as well as those verses which are allegorical.

They are the people of al-Dhikr whom the Messenger of Allah equated with the Holy Qur'an in his saying "the two weighty things" (al-Thaqalayn), and ordered us to adhere to them[1], He equated them to Noah's Ark: whoever joined it was saved, and whoever left it drowned[2]. The Companions knew the position of Ahl al-Bayt and revered them and respected them. The Shi'a follow them and put them above any of the Companions, and to support that they have many clear texts as proofs.

The Sunnis respect and revere the Companions but do not accept the above classification and do not believe that some of the Companions were hypocrites; rather, they see the Companions as being the best people after the Messenger of Allah. If they classify the Companions then it would be according to their seniority and their merits and their services to Islam. They put the Rightly Guided Caliphs in the first class, then the first six of the ten who were promised with heaven, according to them. Therefore when they pray for the Prophet (saw) and his household they attach with them all the Companions without exception.

This is what I know from the Sunni scholars, and that is what I heard from the Shi'i scholars regarding the classification of the Companions; and that is what made me start my detailed study with the issue of the

Companions. I promised my God - if He led me on the right path - to rid myself from emotional bias and to be neutral and objective and to listen to what the two sides said, then to follow what was best, basing my conclusions on two premises:

1. A sound and a logical premise: that is to say that I would only depend upon what everybody is in agreement with, regarding the commentary on the Book of Allah, and the correct parts of the honorable Sunnah of the Prophet.
2. The mind: for it is the greatest gift that Allah has given to human beings, and through it He honored them and distinguished them from the rest of creation. Thus, when Allah protests about what His worshippers do, He asks them to use their minds in the best possible way, and He says: Do they not understand? Do they not comprehend? Do they not see? etc."

Let my Islam primarily be the belief in Allah, His angels, His Books and His messengers; and that Muhammad is His servant and His Messenger; and that the Religion of Allah is Islam; and that I will never depend on any of the Companions, regardless of his relation to the Messenger or his position, for I am neither Umayyad nor Abbasid nor Fatimid, and I am neither Sunni nor Shi'i, and I have no enmity towards Abu Bakr or Umar or Uthman or 'Ali or even Wahshi, the killer of our master al-Hamzah, as long as he became a Muslim, and the Messenger of Allah forgave him. Since I had forced myself into this study in order to reach the truth, and since I had rid myself, sincerely, from all my previous beliefs, I decided to start, with the blessing of Allah, by considering the attitudes of the Companions.

Notes

1. Kanz al Ummal, vol 1 p 44, Ahmed's Musnad, vol 5 p 182
2. al Mustadrak, al Hakim (al Dhahabi's abridged), vol 3 p 151, Al Sawaiq al Muhriqah, Ibn Hajjar, p 184, 234

The Companions at the Peace Treaty of al Hudaibiyah

Briefly the story is as follows: In the sixth year after the Hijrah (emigration of the Prophet from Mecca to Madinah), the Messenger of Allah with one thousand and four hundred of his Companions marched towards Mecca to do the Umrah. They camped in "Dhi al-Halifah" where the Prophet (saw) ordered his Companions to put down their arms and wear the Ihram (white gowns worn especially for the purpose of the pilgrimage and the Umrah), then they dispatched al-Hady (an offering for sacrifice) to inform Quraysh that he was coming as a visitor to do the Umrah and not as a fighter.

But Quraysh, with all its arrogance, feared that its reputation would be dented if the other Arabs heard that Muhammad had entered Mecca by force. Therefore, they sent a delegation led by Suhayl ibn Amr ibn Abd Wadd al-Amiri to see the Prophet and ask him to turn back that year, but said that they would allow him to visit Mecca for three days the year after. In addition to that, they put down some harsh conditions, which were accepted by the Messenger of Allah as the circumstances warranted such acceptance, and as revealed to him by his God, Glory and Might be to Him. A few of the Companions did not like the Prophet's action and opposed him very strongly, and Umar ibn al-Khattab came and said to him, "Are you not truly the Prophet of Allah?" He answered, "Yes, I am." Umar asked, "Are we not right and our enemy wrong?" The Prophet answered, "Yes."

Umar asked, "Why do we then disgrace our religion?"

The Messenger of Allah (saw) said, "I am the Messenger of Allah and I will never disobey Him and He is my support." Umar asked, "Did you not tell us that we would come to the House of Allah and go around it?" The Prophet answered, "Yes, and did I tell you that we were coming this year?" Umar answered, "No." The Prophet said, "Then you are coming to it and going around it." Umar later went to Abu Bakr and asked him, "O Abu Bakr, is he not truly the Prophet of Allah?" He answered, "Yes." Umar then asked him the same questions he had asked the Messenger of Allah, and Abu Bakr answered him with the same answers and added, "O Umar he is the Messenger of Allah, and he will not disobey his God, Who is his support, so hold on to him."

When the Prophet had finished signing the treaty, he said to his Companions "Go and slaughter (sacrifices) and shave your heads." And by Allah one of them stood up until he had said it three times. When nobody obeyed his orders, he went to his quarters, then came out and spoke to no one, and slaughtered a young camel with his own hands, and then asked his barber to shave his head. When the Companions saw all that, they went and slaughtered (sacrifices), and shaved one another, until they nearly killed one another.[1]

This is the summary of the story of peace treaty of al-Hudaibiyah, which is one of the events whose details both the Shi'a and Sunnah agree upon, and it is cited by many historians and biographers of the Prophet such as al- Tabari, Ibn al-Athir, Ibn Saad, al-Bukhari and Muslim.

I stopped here, for I could not read this kind of material without feeling rather surprised about the behavior of those Companions towards their Prophet. Could any sensible man accept some people's claims that the Companions, may Allah bless them, always obeyed and implemented the orders of the Messenger of Allah (saw), for these incidents expose their lies, and fall short of what they want! Could any sensible man imagine that such behavior towards the Prophet is an easy or acceptable matter or even an excusable one! Allah, the Almighty, said:

"But no! By your God! They do not believe (in reality) until they make you a judge of that which has become a matter of disagreement among them, and then do not and any straightness in their hearts as to what you have decided and submit with entire submission." (Holy Qur'an 4:65)

Did Umar ibn al-Khattab succumb to them and find no difficulty in accepting the order of the Messenger (saw)? Or was he reluctant to accept the order of the Prophet? Especially when he said, "Are you not truly the Prophet of Allah? Did you not tell us? Etc." and did he succumb after the Messenger of Allah gave him all these convincing answers?

No, he was not convinced by his answers, and he went and asked Abu Bakr the same questions. But did he succumb after Abu Bakr answered him and advised him to hold on to the Prophet? I do not know if he actually succumbed to all that and was convinced by the answers of the Prophet (saw) and Abu Bakr! For why did he say about himself, "For that I did so many things..." Allah and His Messenger know the things which were done by Umar.

Furthermore, I do not know the reasons behind the reluctance of the rest of the Companions after that, when the Messenger of Allah said to him, "Go and slaughter (sacrifices) and shave your heads." Nobody listened to his orders even when he repeated them three times, and then in vain.

Allah, be praised! I could not believe what I had read. Could the Companions go to that extent in their treatment of the Messenger? If the story had been told by the Shi'a alone, I would have considered it a lie directed towards the honorable Companions. But the story has become so well known that all the Sunni historians refer to it.

As I had committed myself to accept what had been agreed on by all parties, I found myself resigned and perplexed. What could I say? What excuse could I find for those Companions who had spent nearly twenty years with the Messenger of Allah, from the start of the Mission to the day of al-Hudaibiyah, and had seen all the miracles and enlightenment of the Prophethood? Furthermore the Qur'an was teaching them day and night how they should behave in the presence of the Messenger, and how they should talk to him, to the extent that Allah had threatened to ruin their deeds if they raised their voices above his voice.

Note

1. Sahih, Bukhari, Book of al Shurut, Chapter: Al Shurut fi al Jihad vol 2 p 122

The Companions and the Raziyat Yawm al Khamis (The Calamity of Thursday)

Briefly the story is as follows:
The Companions were meeting in the Messenger's house, three days before he died. He ordered them to bring him a bone and an ink pot so that he could write a statement for them which would prevent them from straying from the right path, but the Companions differed among themselves and some of them disobeyed the Prophet and accused him of talking nonsense. The Messenger of Allah became very angry and ordered them out of his house without issuing any statement.

This is the story in some details:

Ibn Abbas said: Thursday, and what a Thursday that was! The Messenger's pain became very severe, and he said, "Come here, I will write you a document which will prevent you from straying from the right path." But Umar said that the Prophet was under the spell of the pain, and that they had the Qur'an which was sufficient being the Book of Allah. Ahl al-Bayt then differed and quarreled amongst themselves, some of them agreeing with what the Prophet said, while others supported Umar's view. When the debate became heated and the noise became louder, the Messenger of Allah said to them, "Leave me alone."

Ibn Abbas said: "The disaster was that the disagreement among the Companions prevented the Messenger from writing that document for them."[1]

The incident is correct and there is no doubt about its authenticity, for it was cited by the Shi'i scholars and their historians in their books, as well as by the Sunni scholars and historians in their books. As I was committed to consider the incident, I found myself bewildered by Umar's behavior regarding the order of the Messenger of Allah. And what an order it was! "To prevent the nation from going astray", for undoubtedly that statement would have had something new in it for the Muslims and would have left them without a shadow of doubt.

Now let us leave the points of view of the Shi'a, that is that the Messenger wanted to write the name of 'Ali as his successor, and that Umar realized this, so he prevented it. Perhaps because they do not convince us initially with that hypothesis, but can we find a sensible explanation to this hurtful incident which angered the Messenger so much that he ordered them to leave, and made Ibn Abbas cry until he made the stones wet from his tears and called it a "great disaster"? The Sunnis say that Umar recognized that the Prophet's illness was advancing, so he wanted to comfort him and relieve him from any pressure.

This type of reasoning would not be accepted by simple-minded people, let alone by the scholars. I repeatedly tried to find an excuse for Umar but the circumstances surrounding the incident prevented me from finding an excuse. Even if I changed the words "He is talking nonsense", God forbid, to "the pain has overcome him", I could not find any justification for Umar when he said, "You have the Qur'an, and it is sufficient being the Book of Allah."

Did he know the Qur'an better than the Messenger of Allah, for whom it was revealed? Or was the Messenger of Allah, God forbid, unaware of what he was? Or did he seek, through his order, to create division and disagreement among the Companions, God forbid.

Even if the Sunni reasoning was right, then the Messenger of Allah would have realized the good will of Umar and thanked him for that and perhaps asked him to stay, instead of feeling angry at him and telling them to leave his house. May I ask why did they abide by his order when he asked them to leave the room and did not say then that he was "talking nonsense"? Was it because they had succeeded in their plot to prevent the Prophet from writing the document, so that there was no need for them to stay any longer? Thus, we find them creating noise and difference in the presence of the Messenger, and divided into two parties: one agreeing with the Messenger of Allah about writing that document, while the other agreed with Umar "that he was talking nonsense."

The matter is not just concerned with Umar alone, for if it was so, the Messenger of Allah would have persuaded him that he could not be talking nonsense and that the pain could not overcome him in matters of the nation's guidance and of preventing it from going astray. But the situation became much more serious, and Umar found some supporters who seemingly had a prior agreement on their stand, and so they created the noise and the disagreement among themselves and forgot, or perhaps pretended to forget, the words of Allah, the Most High:

> *"O You who believe! Do not raise your voices above the voice of the Prophet, and do not speak loud to him as you speak loud to one another, lest your deeds become null while you do not perceive." (Holy Qur'an 49:2)*

In this incident they went beyond raising their voices and talking loud to accusing the Messenger of Allah of talking nonsense, God forbid, then they increased their noise and differences until it became a battle of words in his presence.

I think the majority of the Companions were with Umar, and that is why the Messenger of Allah found it useless to write the document, because he knew that they would not respect him and would not abide by the command of Allah by not raising their voices in his presence, and if they were rebellious against the command of Allah, then they would never obey the order of His Messenger.

Thus, the wisdom of the Messenger ruled that he was not to write the document because it had been attacked during his lifetime, let alone after his death.

The critics would say that he was talking nonsense, and perhaps they would doubt some of the orders he passed whilst on his death-bed, for they were convinced that he was talking nonsense.

I ask Allah for forgiveness, and renounce what has been said in the presence of the holy Messenger, for how could I convince myself and my free conscience that Umar ibn al-Khattab was acting spontaneously, whereas his friends and others who were present at the incident cried until their tears wet the stones, and named the incident "the misfortune of the Muslims". I therefore decided to reject all the justifications given to explain the incident, and even tried to deny it so that I could relax and forget about the tragedy, but all the books referred to it and accepted its authenticity but could not provide sound justification for it.

I tend to agree with the Shi'i point of view in explaining the incident because I find it logical and very coherent.

I still remember the answer which al-Sayyid Muhammad Baqir al-Sadr gave me when I asked him, "How did our master Umar understand, among all the Companions what the Messenger wanted to write, namely the appointment of 'Ali as his successor, as you claim, which shows that he was a clever man?"

Al-Sayyid al-Sadr said: Umar was not the only one who anticipated what the Messenger was going to write. In fact most of the people who were present then understood the situation the same way as Umar did, because the Messenger of Allah had previously indicated the issue when he said, "I shall leave you with two weighty things: the Book of Allah and the members of my Family (Ahl al-Bayt) and their descendants, if you follow them, you will never go astray after me."

And during his illness he said to them, "Let me write you a document, if you follow its contents, you will never go astray." Those who were present, including Umar, understood that the Messenger of Allah wanted to reiterate, in writing, what he had already said in Ghadir Khum, and that was to follow the Book of Allah and Ahl al-Bayt and that 'Ali was the head of it. It was as if the holy Prophet (saw) was saying, "Follow the Qur'an and 'Ali." He said similar things on many occasions, as has been stated by many historians.

The majority of Quraysh did not like 'Ali because he was young and because he smashed their arrogance and had killed their heroes; but they did not dare oppose the Messenger of Allah, as they had done at the Treaty of al-Hudaibiyah, and when the Messenger prayed for Abdullah ibn Abi al- Munafiq, and on many other incidents recorded by history. This incident was one of them, and you see that the opposition against writing that document during the Prophets illness encouraged some of those who were present to be insolent and make so much noise in his presence.

That answer came in accordance with what the saying meant. But Umar's statement, "You have the Qur'an, and it is sufficient, being the Book of Allah" was not in accordance with the saying which ordered them to follow the Book of Allah and the Household (Ahl al-Bayt) together. It looks as if he meant to say, "We have the Book of Allah, and that is sufficient for us, therefore there is no need for Ahl al-Bayt."

I could not see any other reasonable explanation to the incident other than this one, unless it was meant to say, 'Obey Allah but not His Messenger." And this argument is invalid and not sensible. If I put my prejudices and my emotions aside and base my judgment on a clean and free mind, I would tend towards the first analysis, which stops short of accusing Umar of being the first one to reject the Prophet's Tradition (al-Sunnah) when he said, "It is sufficient for us, being the Book of Allah."

Then if there were some rulers who rejected the Prophet's Traditions claiming that it was "contradictory", they only followed an earlier example

in the history of Islam. However, I do not want to burden Umar alone with the responsibility for that incident and the subsequent deprivation of the nation of the guidance. To be fair to him, I suggest that the responsibility should be borne by him and those Companions who were with him and who supported him in his opposition to the command of the Messenger of Allah. I am astonished by those who read this incident and feel as if nothing happened, despite that it was one of the "great misfortunes" as Ibn Abbas called it. My astonishment is even greater regarding those who try hard to preserve the honor of a Companion and to correct his mistake, even if at the cost of the Prophet's dignity and honor and at the cost of Islam and its foundations.

Why do we escape from the truth and try to obliterate it when it is not in accordance with our whims…why do not we accept that the Companions were human like us, and had their own whims, prejudices and interests, and could commit mistakes or could be right?

But my astonishment fades when I read the Book of Allah in which He tells us the stories of the prophets- may Allah bless them and grant them peace - and the disobedience they faced from their people despite all the miracles they produced. Our God! Make not our hearts to deviate after thou hast guided us aright, and grant us from Your Mercy;

surely You are the Most Liberal Giver.

I began to understand the background to the Shi'a's attitude towards the second Caliph, whom they charge with the responsibility for many tragic events in the history of Islam, starting from "Raziyat Yawm al-Khamis" when the Islamic nation was deprived of the written guidance which the Messenger wanted to write for them. The inescapable fact is that the sensible man who knew the truth before he encountered the men seeks an excuse for the Shias in this matter, but there is nothing we can say to convince those who only judge truth through men.

Note

1. Sahih, Bukhari, Chapter: About the saying of the sick, vol 2, Sahih, Muslim, End of the book of al Wasiyyah, vol 5 p 75, Musnad, Ahmed, vol 1 p 335, vol 5 p 116 Tarikh, Tabari, vol 3 p 193, Tarikh, Ibn al Athir, vol 2 p 320

The Companions in the Military Detachment under Usamah

The story in brief is as follows: The Prophet (saw) organized an army to be sent to Asia Minor two days before his death. He appointed Usamah ibn Zayd ibn Haritha, (who was eighteen years old), as its commander in chief, then the holy Prophet attached some important men, both MuHajjireen and Ansar, to this expedition, such as Abu Bakr, Umar, Abu Obaydah and other well-known Companions.

Some people criticized the Prophet for appointing Usamah as the commander in chief of that army, and asked how could he have appointed so young a man as their commander. In fact the same people had previously criticized the Prophet for appointing Usamah's father as an army commander before him. They went on criticizing until the Prophet became so angry that he left his bed, feverish and with his head bandaged, with two men supporting him and his feet barely touching the ground (may my parents be sacrificed for him).

He ascended the pulpit, praised Allah highly then said, "O People! I have been informed that some of you object to my appointing Usamah as commander of the detachment. You now object to my appointing

Usamah as commander in chief as you objected to me appointing his father commander in chief before him. By Allah, his father was certainly competent for his appointment as commander in chief and his son is also competent for the appointment."[1]

Then he exhorted them to start without further delay and kept saying, "Send the detachment of Usamah; deploy the detachment of Usamah, send forward the detachment of Usamah." He kept repeating the exhortations but the Companions were still sluggish, and camped by al-Jurf.

Events like that made me ask, "What is this insolence towards Allah and His Messenger? Why all that disobedience towards the orders of the blessed Messenger who was so caring and kind to all the believers?"

I could not imagine, nor indeed could anybody else, an acceptable explanation for all that disobedience and insolence. As usual, when I read about those events which touch on the integrity of the Companions, I try to deny or ignore them, but it is impossible to do so when all the historians and scholars, Shi'a and Sunnis, agree on their authenticity.

I have promised my God to be fair, and I shall never be biased in favor of my creed, and will never use anything but the truth as my criterion. But the truth here is so bitter, and the holy Prophet (s.a.w.) said, "Say the truth even if it is about you, and say the truth even if it is bitter..." The truth in this case is that the Companions who criticized the appointment of Usamah disobeyed all the clear texts that could not be doubted or misinterpreted, and there is no excuse for that, although some people make flimsy excuses in order to preserve the integrity of the Companions and "the virtuous ancestors".

But the free and sensible person would not accept such feeble excuses, unless he is one of those who cannot comprehend any saying, or is perhaps one of those who are blinded by their own prejudice to the extent that they cannot differentiate between the obligatory task that must be obeyed and the prohibition that must be avoided. I thought deeply to find an acceptable excuse for those people, but without success.

I read the points of view of the Sunnis which provide us with an excuse based on the fact that these people were the elders of Quraysh, and were among the early followers of Islam, whereas Usamah was a young man who had not fought in the decisive battles that gave Islam its glory, such as Badr, Uhud and Hunayn; and that he was a young man with no experience of life when the Messenger of Allah appointed him military commander. Furthermore, they thought that human nature, by its inclination, makes it difficult for elderly people to be led by young men, therefore they (i.e. the Companions) criticized the appointment and wanted the Messenger of Allah to appoint a prominent and respectable Companion.

It is an excuse which is not based on any rational or logical premise, and any Muslim who reads the Qur'an and understands its rules must reject such an excuse, because Allah- the Almighty - says:

"Whatever the Messenger gives you, accept it, and from whatever he forbids you, keep back." (Holy Qur'an 59:7)

"And it behooves not a believing man and a believing woman that they should have any choice in their matter when Allah and His Messenger have decided a matter; and whoever disobeys Allah and His Messenger, he surely strays off a manifest straying." (Holy Qur'an 33:36)

So what kind of an excuse could any rational person accept after reading all these clear texts, and what can I say about people who angered the Messenger of Allah, when they knew that the Messenger's anger is Allah's anger. They accused him of talking "nonsense", and they shouted and disagreed in his presence when he was ill (may my parents be sacrificed for him), until he ordered them to leave his room.

That did not seem to be enough for them, and instead of returning to the right path and asking Allah's forgiveness for what they had done to His Messenger, and asking the Messenger for forgiveness as the Qur'an taught them, they went on criticizing him, despite all the care and kindness he had for them. They did not appreciate him or respect him, and two days after having accused him of talking "nonsense", they criticized him for appointing Usamah as military commander.

They forced him to come out in the appalling condition which the historians describe. Due to the severity of his illness, he had to walk with the support of two men, and then he had to swear by Allah that Usamah was a competent commander for the army.

Furthermore, the Messenger informed us that they had criticized him previously for appointing his father as a commander, which indicates that these people had had many previous confrontations with him, and that they were not willing to obey his orders or accept his judgment, rather, they were prepared to oppose him and confront him, even if such behavior went against the rules of Allah and His Messenger.

What leads us to believe that there was open opposition (to the orders of the Prophet), was that in spite of all the anger shown by the Messenger of Allah, and the fact that he himself tied the flag with his noble hand to the post and commanded them to march immediately, they were sluggish and reluctant to move, and did not go until he had died (may my parents be sacrificed for him). The Prophet (s.a.w.) died feeling sorry for his unfortunate nation, which he feared would go backwards and end up in hell, and no one would be saved except a few, and the Messenger of Allah described them as a handful.

I am surprised that those Companions angered the Prophet on that Thursday and accused him of talking "nonsense", and said, "It is sufficient for us that we have the Book of Allah," when the Holy Qur'an states:

> *"Say if you love Allah, then follow me and Allah will love you." (Holy Qur'an 3:31)*

As if they were more knowledgeable about the Book of Allah and its rules than he to whom it had been revealed. There they were, two days after that great misfortune, and two days before he (the holy Prophet) went up to meet his High Companion, angering him even more by criticizing him for appointing Usamah, and not obeying his orders.

Whereas he was ill and bed-ridden in the first misfortune, in the second one he had to come out, with his head bandaged and covered by a blanket and supported by two men with his feet barely on the ground, and address them from the top of the pulpit. He started his speech with the profession of the unity of Allah and praised Him in order to make them feel that he was not talking nonsense, and then he informed them about what he knew regarding their criticism of his orders.

Furthermore, he reminded them of an incident which had occurred four years previously, in which he was criticized by them. After all that, did they really think that he was talking nonsense or that his illness had overcome him so that he was unaware of what he was saying?

Praise and thanks be to You, Allah, how did these people dare oppose Your Messenger? They disagreed with him when he signed the peace treaty, they opposed him very strongly even when he ordered them to make the sacrifice and shave their heads, and even repeated it three times although no one cared to obey; and again they pulled him by his shirt to prevent him from praying for Abdullah ibn Ubay and said to him, "Allah forbade you from praying for the hypocrites!" As if they were teaching him what had been revealed to him, when You said in

Your Holy Qur'an:

"We have revealed to you the reminder that you may make clear to men what has been revealed to them." (Holy Qur'an 16:44)

And You said:

"We have revealed the Book to you with the truth that you may judge between people by means of that which Allah has taught you."(Holy Qur'an 4:105)

And You said, and Your saying is the truth:

"We have sent among you a messenger from among you who recites to you Our Verses and purifies you and teaches you the Book and the wisdom and teaches you that which you did not know." (Holy Qur'an 2:151)

I am astonished at those people who put themselves in a position higher than that of the Prophet. On one occasion they disobeyed his orders, and on another occasion they accused him of talking nonsense, and then talked loudly and without respect in his presence.

They criticized him for appointing Zayd ibn Harithah to the military command, and after him his son Usamah. How could they leave the scholars in any doubt, after all this evidence, that the Shi'a are right when they put a question mark on the position of some of the Companions, and show their resentment towards these positions purely out of respect and love for the Messenger and the members of his Household.

I have mentioned only four or five of these controversial issues to be brief and to use them as examples, but the Shi'i scholars could recount hundreds of situations in which the Companions contradicted the clear texts. In all this the Shi'a refer to sources written in books by Sunni scholars.

When I look at a number of positions taken by a few of the Companions with regard to the Messenger of Allah, I stand astonished; not because of the attitudes of those Companions alone, but because of the position of the Sunni scholars who gave us the impression that the Companions were always right and could not be criticized. Thus they prevented any researcher from reaching the truth and left him puzzled in the midst of all these contradictions.

In addition to the examples that I have mentioned above, I will bring some more in order to establish a better picture of those Companions, so that we may understand the position of the Shi'a towards them.

According to al-Bukhari in his Sahih, Vol. 4 Page 47, section "The virtue of Patience when one is hurt" and the words of the Almighty "...And those who are patient, surely they will be rewarded," in the Book of Conduct he said:

"Al-Amash told us that he heard Shaqiq saying that Abdullah told him: 'Once the Holy Prophet divided something among a group of men, as he used to do, when one man from al-Ansar stood up and said, 'This division is not for the sake of Allah.' I said, 'For my part, I shall have a word with the Prophet (s.a.w.).' So I went to see him, and I found him with his Companions. I explained my grievances, and the Prophet's face changed and showed signs of anger, and I wished that I had not told him, and then he said: 'Moses was hurt more than that but he was patient.'"

Al-Bukhari mentioned in the same book - i.e. the book of Conduct - in the chapter concerning smiling and laughter that Anas ibn Malik was heard saying: "I was walking with the Messenger of Allah (s.a.w) who was wearing a Najrani cloak with a rather thin edge to it, and suddenly a man approached him and pulled harshly at his cloak.

Anas continued: I looked at the side of the Prophet (s.a.w.) and noticed that as a result of that harsh pull, the edge of the cloak went up to his shoulder, then the man said, 'O Muhammad, give me some of what you have from Allah's wealth!' The Prophet turned to him and laughed, and then he ordered his Companions to pay him something."

Al-Bukhari also mentioned the following incident in the Book of Conduct and put it in the chapter concerning "He who does not face people with blame", he said: "Aisha said that the Prophet (s.a.w.) did something and made it permissible, but no one followed what the Prophet did. The

Prophet (s.a.w.) happened to hear about it, so he decided to address the people. He first thanked Allah then said: 'What is the matter with people who refrain from the thing I did? By Allah, I know more than any of them about Allah, and I fear Him most...!'

When we look deeply at incidents like those above we find that the Companions put themselves on a higher level than the Prophet, and thought that he was wrong and they were right. Furthermore, there were some historians who deliberately corrected the position of the Companions, even if that contradicted the action taken by the Prophet, and showed them at a level of knowledge and piety higher than that of the Prophet.

As is the case when they judge the Prophet wrong in the case of the Prisoners of War at the battle of Badr, so it appears that Umar ibn al-Khattab was right. They also tell wrong stories, such as the following saying attributed to the people: If Allah decided to inflict a disaster on us; no one will escape except Ibn al-Khattab. In other words, they were saying, "If it was not for Umar, the Prophet would have perished." God protect us from such a corrupt and shameful belief, and he who adheres to this kind of belief is surely far from Islam, and ought to review his thinking or rid himself of the devil.

Allah, the most High, said:

"Have you considered him who takes his low desire for his God and Allah has made him err having knowledge and has set a seal upon his ear and his heart and put a covering upon his eye. Who can then guide him after Allah? Will not they be mindful?" (Holy Qur'an 45:23)

I believe that those who think that the Prophet (s.a.w.) was subject to his emotions to the extent that he deviated from the right path and made a judgment not for the cause of Allah, or those who refrained from doing things which were done by the Messenger of Allah thinking that they were more knowledgeable and more pious than the Messenger, do not deserve any respect or appreciation from the Muslims.

They were put at the same level as the angels, as the best people in the whole of creation after the Messenger of Allah, so that Muslims are obliged to follow them and take them as an example, just because they were the Companions of the Messenger of Allah.

That contradicts the belief of Ahl al-Sunnah, who pray for Muhammad and his family, and then add all the Companions. If Allah, praise be to Him the Most High, appreciated them and put them in their correct position and ordered them to pray for His Messenger and the purified members of his family, they should have submitted and known their place with Allah. Why should we then put them in a position which is higher than they deserve and equate them with those people whom Allah has elevated and preferred above all people?

Let me then conclude that the Umayyads and the Abbasids, who opposed-Ahl al-Bayt and exiled them and killed them with their followers, got the gist of that distinguished position and recognized its danger for them. For if Allah, praise be to Him, would not accept the prayers of a Muslim unless he prays for them (Ahl al-Bayt): how could they justify their opposition to them. Therefore, they attached the Companions to Ahl al-Bayt in order to give the impression to the public that they are equal.

Especially when we know that their masters and dignitaries were Companions who bought some other Companions known to have weak personalities and asked them to distribute fabricated sayings (of the Prophet) in praise of the Companions and the next generation, and in particular those who reached the position of Caliphs (i.e. the Umayyad and Abbasid) and they were the direct reason behind them attaining this position and becoming rulers over all the Muslims.

History is the best witness to what I am saying: Umar ibn al-Khattab, who was well known for his strictness towards his governors whom used to dismiss them on mere suspicions, was quite gentle towards Muawiyah ibn Abi Sufyan and never disciplined him. Muawiyah was appointed by Abu Bakr and confirmed by Umar throughout his life, who never even rebuked him or blamed him, despite the fact that many people complained about Muawiyah and reported him for wearing silk and gold, which was prohibited to men by the Messenger of Allah. Umar used to answer these complaints by saying, "Let him be, he is the Kisra (king) of the Arabs."

Muawiyah continued in the governorship for more than twenty years without being touched or criticized, and when Uthman succeeded to the caliphate of the Muslims, he added to his authority further districts and regions, which enabled him to a mass great wealth from the Islamic nation and to raise armies to rebel against the Imam (Leader) of the nation and subsequently take the full power by force and intimidation. Thus he became the sole ruler of all Muslims, and later forced them to vote for his corrupt and alcohol drinking son Yazid, as his heir and successor.

This is a long story so I will not go into its details in this book, but the important thing is that we should understand the mentality of those

Companions who reached the position of caliph and facilitated the establishment of the Umayyad state in a direct way, so as to please Quraysh which did not want to see both the Prophethood and the caliphate in the House of Bani Hashim.[2]

The Umayyad state had the right, or indeed was obliged to thank those who had facilitated its establishment, most of all the "story tellers" whom it hired to tell tales about the virtues of their masters. In the meantime it elevated them to a higher place than that of their enemies, Ahl al-Bayt, simply by inventing virtues and merits, which if (may Allah witness) examined under the light of logical and legal evidence mostly disappear, unless there is something wrong with our minds or we have started believing in contradictions.

For example, we hear so much about Umar's justice which the "storytellers" attributed to him. It was even said about him "You ruled with justice, therefore you can sleep." It has also been said that Umar was buried in a standing position so that justice would not die with him...and you could go on and on talking about Umar's justice.

However, the correct history tells us that when Umar ordered that grants should be distributed among the people during the twentieth year of al- Hijrah, he did not follow the tradition of the Messenger of Allah, nor did he confine himself to its rules. The Prophet (s.a.w.) distributed the grants on an equal basis among all Muslims and did not differentiate between one person and another, and Abu Bakr did the same throughout his caliphate.

But Umar introduced a new method. He preferred the early converts to Islam to those who came later. He preferred al-MuHajjireen (immigrants from Mecca to Medinah) from Quraysh to other MuHajjireen. He preferred all the MuHajjireen to al-Ansar (followers of Prophet Muhammad in Medinah who granted him refuge after the Hijra). He preferred the Arabs to the non-Arabs. He preferred the freeman to the slave.[3] He preferred (the tribe of) Mudar to (the tribe of) Rabia for he gave three hundred to the former and two hundred to the latter.⁴ He also preferred al-Aws to al-Khazraj.⁵

Where is the justice in all this differentiation, O people who have minds? We also hear so much about Umar's knowledge, to the extent he was described as the most knowledgeable Companion, and it has been said about him that he agreed with his God on many ideas that were revealed in various Qur'anic verses, and that he disagreed with the Prophet about them. But the correct history tells us that Umar did not agree with the Qur'an, even after it had been revealed.

When one of the Companions asked him one day during his caliphate, "O Commander of the Believers, I am unclean, but I cannot find water to wash." Umar answered, "Do not pray." Then Ammar ibn Yasir had to remind him about Tayammum (ritual cleaning with earth), but Umar was not convinced, and said to Ammar, "You are responsible only for the duties which have been assigned to you."⁶

Where is Umar's knowledge regarding the Tayammum verse which had been revealed in the Book of Allah, and where is Umar's knowledge of the Tradition of the Prophet (s.a.w.) who taught them how to do Tayammum as well as Wudu (ritual ablution). Umar himself confessed on many occasions that he was not a scholar, and that all people, even women were more knowledgeable than him, and he was heard saying many times, "If it was not for 'Ali, Umar would have perished." And throughout his life he did not know the rule of al-Kalalah (relatives of the dead excluding the son and the father), although he passed various different judgments about it, as history witnesses.

We also hear a great deal about the courage and physical strength of Umar, and it has been said that Quraysh feared the day when Umar became a Muslim, and that Islam became even stronger when he entered the religion. It has also been said that Allah glorified Islam with Umar, and that the Messenger of Allah did not call for Islam openly until after Umar had become a Muslim.

But the correct historical references do not seem to indicate that courage, and history does not mention one famous or even ordinary person who has been killed by Umar in a dual or a battle like Badr and Uhud or al-Khandaq. In fact the correct historical references tell us exactly the opposite; they tell us that he escaped with the fugitives in Uhud, and escaped on the day of Hunayn, and that when the Messenger of Allah sent him to take the city of Khayber he returned defeated. He was never even the leader in the military detachments in which he served and in the last one (that of Usamah) he was put under the charge of young Usamah ibn Zayd. So where is all that courage compared to these historical facts…O people who have minds?

We also hear about Umar's piety and his great fear of Allah, to the extent of crying. It has been said that he was afraid of being accountable before Allah if a mule tumbled in Iraq because he did not pave the road for it. But the correct historical sources tell us that he was a rough man who lacked piety and did not hesitate to beat a man until he bled because he asked him about a Qur'anic verse, and even that women used to miscarry their babies out of fear when they saw him. Why did he not fear Allah when he raised his sword and threatened anybody who said that Muhammad had died, and he swore by Allah that he had not died, rather, he had gone to talk to his God in the same way as Moses did. Then he threatened to kill whoever said that Muhammad was dead.[7]

Why did he not fear Allah when he threatened to burn Fatimah al-Zahra's house if those who refrained from voting for the successorship of the caliphate did not come out?[8] It has been said that when he was told that Fatimah was inside, he answered, "So what!" He violated the Book of Allah and the Tradition of the Prophet and passed rules and judgments during his caliphate which contradicted the texts of the Holy Qur'an and the noble Tradition of the Prophet (s.a.w.).[9]

So where was all that piety and fear of Allah in all these bitter and sad historical facts, O good worshippers of Allah? I took this great and famous Companion as an example, and I have summarized a great deal to avoid prolongation, but if I wanted to talk in some detail, I could have filled many volumes. But as I said I have mentioned these historical references as examples and not for specific reasons.

What I have mentioned is a small amount, but it gives us a clear indication as to the mentalities of the Companions and the contradictory attitudes of the Sunni scholars and historians. For on the one hand they forbid people from criticizing them or doubting their intentions, but on the other hand they write in their books things that make people doubt their deeds and criticize them.

I wish the Sunni scholars had not written about these matters in such a way that it clearly sullies the dignity of the Companions and ruins their integrity. If they had not we would have been spared all that confusion.

I still remember meeting a scholar from al-Najaf whose name was Asad Hayder (author of "Al-lmam al-Sadiq wa al- Madhahib al-Arbaah") and as we were talking about the Sunnis and the Shi'a he told me a story about his father. He (i.e. the father) had met a Tunisian scholar from al-Zaytunah during the pilgrimage season some fifty years ago, and started a debate about the Imamate of 'Ali - may Allah's peace be upon him - and his eligibility to the succession for the caliphate. The Tunisian scholar listened attentively as the other man mentioned four or five reasons. When he had finished, the scholar from al-Zaytunah asked him, "Have you got any other reasons?" The man answered, "No." Then the Tunisian scholar said, "Get your rosary out and start counting, then he listed some hundred reasons that my father had not known before."

Shaykh Asad Hayder added, "If the Sunnis read what is in their books, then they would say similar things to what we are saying and we would not have any differences between us for a long time."

By my life! It is the inevitable truth, if only man would liberate himself from his blind prejudice and his arrogance and submit to the clear proof.

Notes

1. Al-Tabaqat by Ibn Sa'ad Vol.; Tarikh Ibn al-Athir Vol. 2 page 317; Al-Sirah al- Halabiyah Vol. 3 page 207; Tarikh al-Tabari Vol. 3 page 226
2. For more detail read: Al-Khilafah wa al-mulk by Abu al Aala al-Mawdudi.; Yawm al-Islam by Ahmed Amin.
3. Sharh Ibn Abi al-Hadid Vol. 8 page 111.
4. Tarikh al-Ya'qubi Vol.2 page 106.
5. Futuh al-Buldan page 437.
6. Sahih al-Bukhari Vol. 1 page 52.
7. Tarikh al-Tabari and Tarikh Ibn al-Athir.
8. Al-Imamah wal Siyasah by Ibn Qutaybah.
9. See Al-Nas wal-Ijtihad by Abdul Husayn Sharaf al-Din.

The Opinion of the Quran regarding the Companions

First of all, I must say that Allah - praise be to Him the Most High - commended, in many places in His Holy Book, the Companions of the Messenger of Allah who loved, obeyed, and followed the Messenger without personal greed and without opposition or arrogance, and only wanted the acceptance of Allah and His Messenger; those Companions have pleased Allah and He pleased them, and that is the way for those who fear Allah.

This group of the Companions are appreciated by the Muslims because of their attitude towards the Prophet (saw) and their works with him, therefore they are liked and respected by all Muslims, and they are appreciated whenever people mention their names.

My study does not concern itself with this group of Companions who are respected by both the Sunnis and the Shi'a, nor is it concerned, with those who were well known for their hypocrisy, and who are cursed by all Muslims, Shi'a and Sunnis, whenever their names are mentioned.

However, my study is concerned with the group of Companions about whom the Muslims have expressed different views. There are verses in the Holy Qur'an where they are rebuked and threatened because of their attitudes in certain positions, and the Messenger of Allah (saw) warned them on many occasions, and warned other people about them.

The outstanding differences between the Shi'a and the Sunnis is concerned with this group of Companions, because the Shi'a criticize their sayings and deeds and complain about their justice, whereas they are respected by the Sunnis, in spite of their contradictions. My study is concerned with this group of the Companions because through it I will be able to reach the truth, or part of it. I say that, so that no one may think that I have neglected the Qur'anic verses which commend the Companions to the Messenger of Allah, and that I exposed the verses which criticize them. In fact through my research I discovered that some verses contain praise for the Companions, but if you read in between the lines you find that they contain criticism of them, and vice versa.

I shall not write here about all the hard work that I have done in the past three years in preparing this study, but I will confine myself to some Qur'anic verses as examples, and not for any specific reason. For those who want to go further, I advise them to research and compare, as I did, in order that they may find the Right Faith by themselves, and through their own work. That is what Allah wants for everybody, and that is what the conscience of each individual wants. Thus, one would achieve an absolute conviction that will not be shaken by any storm. After all, the divine guidance which results from personal conviction is far better than that which comes as a result of external factors.

Allah - the Most High says in praise of His Prophet (saw):

"And found you unable to see (the way) then He showed you the way" (Holy Qur'an 93:7).

That is He found you searching for the truth, so He led you to it. He also said:

> *"And those who strive hard for Us, We will guide them in Our ways"* (Holy Qur'an 29:69).

The turning back verse

Allah - the Most High says in His Glorious Book:

> *"And Muhammad is no more than a messenger, the messengers have already passed away before him, if then he dies or is killed, will you turn back upon your heels? And whoever turns back upon his heels, he will by no means do harm to Allah in the least, and Allah will reward the grateful."* Allah, the Great, has told the truth (Holy Qur'an 3:144).

This Qur'anic verse is clear about how the Companions will turn back upon their heels, and only a few will stand their ground, as the above Qur'anic verse indicated in the expression of Allah about them. Those who stand their ground and do not turn back are the grateful, for the grateful are only a small minority, as in the words of Allah- the Most High:

> *"And very few of My servants are grateful"* (Holy Quran 34:13).

Also there are many sayings of the Holy Prophet (saw) which explain the "turning back," and we will refer to some of them, and even if Allah, the Most High, did not specify the punishment of those who turned back on their heels in this Qur'anic verse: He glorified the grateful who deserve His reward. However, it is important to know that those who turned back on their heels do not deserve the reward of Allah and His forgiveness, as has been emphasized by the Messenger of Allah (saw) in many of his sayings, some of we will discuss, if Allah wills, in the course of this book.

We could not explain the Qur'anic verse with reference to Tulayha, Sujah and al-Aswad al-Ansi, out of respect for the Companions, because the above-mentioned Companions have turned back and abandoned Islam, and even claimed the prophecy during the lifetime of the Messenger of Allah, who fought them and finally defeated them.

Nor indeed can we explain the Qur'anic verse with reference to Malik Ibn Nuwayrah and his followers, who refused to pay Zakat (alms) in the time of the caliph Abu Bakr, for many reasons. They refused to pay al-Zakat (alms) and give it to Abu Bakr because they wanted to wait and see what happened, for they had accompanied the Messenger of Allah on his farewell pilgrimage, and voted for Imam 'Ali ibn Abi Talib at Ghadir Khum after the Messenger of Allah appointed him as Caliph after him, and indeed Abu Bakr himself voted for 'Ali.

Therefore, they were astonished when a messenger from the caliph came to tell them the news of the holy Prophet's death and at the same time asked them to pay Zakat in the name the new caliph, Abu Bakr. It is a case in which history does not want to go too deep, for the sake of the Companion's honor.

Furthermore, Malik and his followers were Muslims according to the testimony of Umar and Abu Bakr themselves and other Companions who disapproved of Khalid ibn al-Walid's killing of Malik. History testifies that Abu Bakr paid compensation for Malik's death to his brother Mutammem out of the Muslim's treasury, and apologized for his killing. It is well established that the apostate must be killed, and no compensation be paid out of the Muslim's treasury for his killing, and no apologies issued for killing him.

The important thing is that the "turning back" verse refers to the Companions who lived with the Messenger of Allah in al-Medinah al- Munawwarah, and indicates the immediate "turning back" after the Prophet's death. The Prophet's sayings explain all these things in such a clear way, that no one could doubt it. We shall deal with these matters soon, if Allah wills. History also testifies for the "turning back" that happened after the death of the Messenger of Allah, and when we view the events which took place among the ranks of the Companions we notice that only a few managed to come out unscathed.

The Holy War (Jihad) Verse

Allah, the Most High, said:

> *"O You who believe, what (excuse) have you that when it is said to you: Go forth in Allah's way, you should incline heavily to earth; are you contented with this world's life instead of the Hereafter? But the provision of this world's life compared with the Hereafter is but little. If you do not go forth, He will chastise you with a painful chastisement and bring in your place a people other than you, and you will do Him no harm; and Allah has power over all things"* (Holy Qur'an 9:38-39).

This Qur'anic verse is clear about the reluctance of the Companions to go and fight in the Holy War (Jihad), and how they chose to be content with the life on earth, in spite of their knowledge of its short duration. Their action warranted a rebuke and a threat from Allah - the Almighty - that a terrible torture was awaiting them, and that He would change them for others who were true believers.

The threat to change them came in many Qur'anic verses which indicate clearly that they showed their reluctance to fight in al-Jihad-Holy War - more than once, and Allah, the Most High, says:

> "And if you turn back He will bring in your place another people, they will not be like you" (Holy Qur'an 47:38).

Also the Almighty says:

> "O You who believe! Whoever from among you turns back from his religion, then Allah will bring a people, He shall love them and they shall love Him, lowly before the believers, mighty against the unbelievers, they shall strive hard in Allah's way and shall not fear the censure of any censurer, this is Allah's grace, He gives it to whom He pleases, and Allah is Ample-giving, Knowing" (Holy Qur'an 5:54).

If we want to investigate the Qur'anic verses which emphasize this issue and talk about the classification of the Companions, which the Shi'a advocate, then we would need a special book for it. The Holy Qur'an expressed all that in the most direct and eloquent way:

"Let there arise out of you a nation, inviting to all that is good, enjoining what is right, and forbidding what is wrong, and these it is that shall be successful. And be not like those who became divided and disagreed after receiving clear signs and these it is that shall have a grievous chastisement.

> On the day, some faces will be white (lit up) and some faces will be black (in the gloom), to those whose faces will be black (will be said): Did you reject the faith after accepting it? Taste then the chastisement for rejecting the faith. But those whose faces will be white, they will be in Allah's mercy,

therein to dwell" (Holy Qur'an 3:106-107).

These Qur'anic verses as every scholar knows are addressing the Companions and warning them of the division and disagreement among themselves after they have already been shown the Right Path. They also tell them that a great torture is awaiting them, and divide them in two groups: The first group: when they will be resurrected on the Day of Judgment, every one of them would have a white face, and those are the grateful who deserve the mercy of Allah. The second group: when they will be resurrected on the Day of Judgment, every one of them would have a black face, and those are the apostates, whom Allah, the Almighty, promised the great torture.

It is well-known that the Companions were divided after the death of the Messenger of Allah. They disagreed among themselves to such an extent that they fought each other bloody wars which led to the regression and the backwardness of the Muslims and made them easy target for their enemies. The above Qur'anic verse could not be interpreted in any other way except that which is readily accepted by people.

The Submissiveness

Allah, the most High, said:

> "Has not the time yet come for those who believe that their hearts should be submissive for the remembrance of Allah and what has come down of the truth? And (that) they should not be like those who were given the book before, but the time became prolonged to them, so their hearts hardened, and most of them are transgressors." (Holy Qur'an 57:16).

In al-Durr al-Manthur by Jalal al-Din al-Suyuti, the author says: "When the Companions of the Messenger of Allah (saw) came to al-Medinah and started to enjoy a higher standard of living after having lived through many hardships, they seemed to slow down, so they were punished for that, and hence the verse 'Has not the time yet come for those who believe' was revealed."

Another version of the story, which came from the Prophet (saw), was that Allah, the Most High, found some reluctance in the MuHajjereen seventeen years after the first revelation of the Holy Qur'an, and therefore Allah revealed the verse "Has not the time yet come for those who believe." If those Companions, who are the best people according to the Sunnis, did not feel humble before the name of Allah or His right revelation of seventeen years, so that Allah found them slowing down, and rebuked and warned them for their hardened hearts which were leading them to corruption, we cannot blame the people of Quraysh who only entered Islam in the seventh Hijri year after the conquest of Makkah.

These were some examples which I have selected from the Glorious Book of Allah which give us clear indications that not all the Companions were right, as the Sunnis believe.

If we study the sayings of the Prophet (saw), then we will find many more examples, but just to be brief, I shall refer to some of those examples and the interested reader may further his own knowledge if he so wishes.

The Opinion of the Messenger regarding the Companions

The hadith of the Pool

The Messenger of Allah (saw) said: "As I was standing, there came a group of people whom I recognized, and a man stood between the group and myself, then said: 'Let us go.' I said, 'Where to?' He said, 'To Hell, by Allah!' I asked, 'What have they done?' He answered, 'They turned back after you had departed, and I expect only a few will reach salvation.'"[1]

The Messenger of Allah (saw) also said: "I shall arrive at the pool before you, and he who passes by me will drink, and whoever drinks from it will never feel thirsty. There will come to me people that I know and they know me, but we shall be separated, then I shall say, ''My companions.' An answer shall come, 'You do not know what they did after you left.' Then I shall say, 'Away with those who changed after me.'"

When we look deeply at the various sayings that have been referred to by the Sunnis in their books, we will have no doubt that most of the

Companions changed or even became apostates after the departure of the Messenger of Allah, except a few who were considered to be the minority. The above sayings could not be applied to the third type (of Companions), for they were the hypocrites, and the text states: "I shall say, 'My companions.'"

These sayings confirm and explain the Holy Qur'anic verses that we mentioned earlier on, which talked about their retreat and their apostasy and the terrible torture awaiting them.

The hadith of the Competition of the World

The Messenger of Allah (saw) said: "I lead you and am your witness, and by Allah I now look at my pool and have been given the keys to the treasures of the earth (for the earth's keys), and by Allah I am not worried that you become polytheist after me, but I am worried that you will compete for it."[2]

The Messenger of Allah (saw) was right. They competed for this world to the extent that they fought against each other, and each party accused the other of blasphemy. Some of the famous Companions were eager to collect gold and silver, and historians such as al-Masudi in Muruj al-Dhahab and al- Tabari and others stated that the wealth of al-Zubayr on its own came to fifty thousand Dinars and a thousand horses with one thousand slaves and many holdings in Basra al-Kufa Egypt and many other places.[3]

The agricultural products from Iraq alone brought Talhah one thousand Dinars every day, and perhaps more than that.

Abdul Rahman ibn Awf had one hundred horses, one thousand camels and ten thousand sheep. After his death, quarter of his wealth which was divided among his wives came to eighty four thousand Dinars.[4]

Uthman ibn Affan left on the day of his death one hundred and fifty thousand Dinars apart from an enormous wealth of land, cattle and villages.

Zayd ibn Thabit left an amount of gold and silver that had to be broken by hammers! Apart from money and agricultural holdings which came to one hundred thousand Dinars.[5]

These were just a few historical examples. Since we do not want to go into detailed analysis of their importance at the moment, we only mentions them as a proof and support of the sayings, that they (these companions) were more interested in the present life.

Notes

1. Sahih, Bukhari, vol 4 p 94-99, 156, vol 3 p 32; Sahih, Muslim, vol 7 p 66
2. Muruj al Dhahab, al Masudi, vol 2 p 341
3. Muruj al Dhahab, al Masudi, vol 2 p 341
4. Muruj al Dhahab, al Masudi, vol 2 p 341
5. Muruj al Dhahab, al Masudi, vol 2 p 341

The Opinion of the Companions about Each Other

1. Their testimony that they themselves have changed the tradition of the Prophet

Abu Saeed al-Khudari said: On the first days of 'Id al-Fitr (breaking the fast of Ramadan) and 'Id al-Adha (celebrating the end of the Pilgrimage), the first thing the Messenger of Allah (saw) used to do was to say his prayers in the mosque, then he went to see the people, who sat in rows in front of him, and then he started to deliver advice or orders or even finalize outstanding issues, and after all that he would leave. Abu Saeed added: The situation continued to be like that, until one day, either Fitr or Adha, I went with Marwan, who was the governor of al-Medinah.

When we arrived at the mosque, which had a new pulpit built by Kathir ibn al-Salt, Marwan headed for the pulpit (before praying), so I pulled him by his clothes, but he pushed me and went up on to the pulpit. He addressed the people before he prayed, so I said to him, "By

Allah you have changed it." He replied, "O Abu Saeed, what you know has gone." I said, 'By Allah, what I know is better than what I do not know.' Marwan then said, 'People did not sit for us after the prayers, so I put (it) before the prayers.'"[1]

I looked for the reasons which led those Companions to change the Sunnah (the tradition) of the Messenger of Allah (saw), and found that the Umayyads (and most of them were Companions of the Prophet) and Muawiah ibn Abi Sufian (writer of the revelation, as he was called) in particular used to force people to swear at 'Ali ibn Abi Talib and curse him from the pulpits of the mosques, as most of the historians have mentioned in their books.

Muslim, in his Sahih, wrote in a chapter entitled, "The virtues of 'Ali ibn Abi Talib," the following: Muawiah ordered his governors everywhere to take the curse (of 'Ali ibn Abi Talib) as tradition, and that all the speakers must include it in their speeches. When some of the Companions protested very strongly against such a rule, Muawiah ordered their killing and burning. Among the famous Companions who were killed at the order of Muawiah were Hijr ibn Adi al-Kindi and his followers, because they protested and refused to curse 'Ali, and some of them were buried alive.

Abu al-Aala al-Mawdudi wrote in his book "Caliphate and Kingdom": Abu al-Hasan al-Basri said: Muawiah had four features, and if he had only one of them, it would have been considered a great sin:

1. Making decisions without consulting the Companions, who were the light of virtues.
2. Designating his son as his successor. His son was a drunkard, corrupt and wore silk.
3. He claimed Ziyad (as his son), and the Messenger of Allah said, "There is offspring for the honorable woman, but there is nothing for the whore."

4. His killing of Hijr and his followers. Woe unto him from Hijr and the followers of Hijr.²

There were some good Companions who used to dash out of the mosque immediately after the prayers so that they did not have to listen to the
speeches which always ended with the cursing of 'Ali. For that reason the Umayyads changed the tradition of the Messenger of Allah. They put the speech before the prayers, so that people listened to it against their will.

What kind of Companions were these people! They were not afraid of changing the tradition of the Messenger of Allah, or even the laws of Allah, in order to reach their wicked and low objectives and to satisfy their sinister desires. They cursed a man whom Allah had kept cleansed and purified, and made it obligatory for people to pray for him in the same way as they prayed for His Messenger. Furthermore, Allah and His Messenger made it obligatory for people to love him, and the Prophet (saw) said, "Loving 'Ali is believing, and hating him is hypocrisy."³

But these Companions changed the rules and said, "We heard, but we disobey." And instead of loving him, praying for him and obeying him, they swore at him and cursed him for sixty years, as has been mentioned in the history books.

Whereas the Companions of Moses plotted against Aaron and tried to kill him, some of the Companions of Muhammad killed his Aaron and pursued his sons and followers everywhere. They removed their names from the Diwan (account books of the treasury) and prohibited anyone to be named after them. As if that was not enough for them, they cursed him and forced the faithful Companions to do so unjustly and by force.

By Allah! I stand astonished and perplexed when I read in our Sihahs how much the Messenger of Allah loved his "brother" and cousin 'Ali and how he put him above all the Companions, and even he said, "You are to me as Aaron was to Moses, but there will be no prophet after me."[4]

He also said the following things about 'Ali:

"You are from me, and I am from you."[5]

"Loving 'Ali is believing, and hating him is hypocrisy."[6] "I am the city of knowledge, and 'Ali is its gate."[7]

"'Ali is the master of all the believers after me."[8]

"Whoever accepted me as his master, then he should also accept 'Ali as his master. O Allah be friendly with his friends, and be enemy to his enemy."[9]

If we study all the virtues that the Prophet (saw) attributed to 'Ali, which have been mentioned and approved by our scholars in their books, then we would need to write a whole book.

So, how did the Companions ignore all these texts, swear at him, plot against him, curse him from the pulpits of the mosques and then fight against him and finally kill him?

I tried in vain to find a reason for the behavior of those people, but found nothing except the love of this life and the competition for it, in addition to the tendency to apostatize and turn back on their heels. I have also tried to attach the responsibility to a group of bad Companions and some hypocrites, but regrettably those were only a few among the famous and the important. The first who threatened to burn his house, with its inhabitants, was Umar ibn al-Khattab, and the first who fought him were Talhah, al-Zubayr, Aishah bint Abi Bakr - Umm al-Mumineen, Muawiah ibn Abi Sufian, Amr ibn al- 'Aas and many others.

I am astonished, and my astonishment will never end, and any responsible free thinker would agree with me, as to how the Sunni scholars agree on the righteousness of all the Companions and ask for the blessings of Allah to be upon them and pray for all of them without exception, although some of them say: "Curse Yazid, and no further." But where is Yazid amongst all these tragedies which no religion or logic could approve? I appeal to the Sunni people, if they truly follow the Prophet's tradition,

to ask themselves how they could accept somebody to be righteous when the laws of the Holy Qur'an and the Prophetic tradition judge him as being corrupt, an apostate and an unbeliever. The Messenger of Allah (saw) said, "He who insults 'Ali, insults me. He, who insults me, insults Allah. And he who insults Allah, Allah will throw him into Hell."[10] If that is the punishment for those who insult 'Ali, one wonders about the punishment of those who fought him and ultimately killed him. What are our scholars' opinions regarding all these facts, or are their hearts locked solid?! Say, O God please protect us from the tricks of the devil.

The Companions even made changes in Prayers

Anas ibn Malik said: I knew nothing during the lifetime of the Prophet (saw) better than the prayer. He said: Have you not lost what you have lost in it? Al-Zuhri said: I went to see Anas ibn Malik in Damascus, and found him crying, I asked him, "What is making you cry?" He answered, "I have known nothing but these prayers and they have been lost."[11]

I would like to make it clear that it was not the followers who implemented the changes after all the intrigues and civil wars, rather it was the caliph Uthman who first made changed in the Prophet's tradition regarding the prayers.

Also Umm al-Mumineen Aishah was involved in these changes. Al-Bukhari and Muslim, both stated in their books that the Messenger of Allah (saw) performed two prayers at Mina, and Abu Bakr after him, then Umar and Uthman who later performed four prayers.[12]

Muslim also stated in his book that al-Zuhri asked 'Urwah, "Why did Aishah complete her prayers during the journey?" He answered, "She improvised in the same way as Uthman did."[13]

Umar used to improvise and interpret the clear texts of the Prophet's tradition, and even the Holy Qur'anic texts. Like he used to say: "Two pleasures were allowed during the life of the Messenger of Allah, but now I disallow them and punish those who commit them and I tell the person who is in a state of ritual impurity or cannot find water not to pray." This in spite of the words of Allah, the Most High, in Surat al-Maidah: "If you do not find water, then use clean sand."

Al-Bukhari stated in his book, in a chapter which deals with ritual impurity: "I heard Shaqiq ibn Salmah saying: 'I was with Abdullah and Abu Musa, and Abu Musa asked, 'What do you say about a man who is unclean but cannot find water?' Abdullah answered, 'He should not pray until he finds water.' Abu Musa then asked, 'what do you think about what the Prophet said to Ammar (regarding the issue of impurity) when Ammar asked him?'

Abdullah said, 'For that reason Umar was not satisfied with (that).' Abu Musa said, 'Forget about what Ammar said, but what do you say about the Qur'anic verse?' Abdullah did not know what to say, but he justified his stance by saying, 'If we let them do that, then whenever the water becomes cold, they avoid using it to clean themselves, and instead they use sand.' I said to Shaqiq, 'Abdullah is most certainly hated for that.' He said, 'Yes.'"[14]

The Companions Testify against themselves

"Anas ibn Malik said that the Messenger of Allah (saw) said to al-Ansar: 'You will notice after me some great selfishness, but be patient until you meet Allah and His Messenger by the pool. Anas said: We were not patient.'¹⁵

"Al-Ala ibn al-Musayyab heard his father saying: 'I met al-Bara ibn Azib, may Allah honor them both, and said to him, 'Bless you, you accompanied the Prophet (saw) and you voted for him under the tree.' He said, 'My son, you do not know what we have done after him.'".¹⁶

This early Companion, who was one of those who voted for the Prophet under the tree, and who received the blessing of Allah, for Allah knew what was in their hearts, testifies against himself and his companions that they did not keep the tradition. This testimony is confirmation of what the Prophet (saw) talked about and predicted in that his Companions would break with his tradition and fall back on their heels.

How could any sensible person, after all this evidence, believe in the righteousness of all the Companions, as the Sunnis do?

He, who believes that, is definitely reversing the order of logic and scholarship, and there will be no intellectual criteria for the researcher to use in his quest for the truth.

The testimony of the Shaykhan against themselves

In a chapter entitled "The virtues of Umar ibn al-Khattab," al-Bukhari wrote in his book: "When Umar was stabbed he felt great pain and Ibn Abbas wanted to comfort him, so he said to him, "O Commander of the Believers, you accompanied the Messenger of Allah and you were a good companion to him, and when he left you, he was very pleased with you.

Then you accompanied Abu Bakr, and you were a good companion to him, and when he left you, he was pleased with you. Then you accompanied their companions and you were a good companion to them, and if you left them, they would remember you well."

He said, "As for the companionship of the Messenger of Allah and his satisfaction with me, that is a gift that Allah, the Most High, has granted to me. As for the companionship of Abu Bakr and his satisfaction with me, that is a gift that Allah, Glory be to Him, has granted to me. But the reason you see me in pain is for you and your companions. By Allah, if I had all the gold on earth I would use it to ransom myself from the torture of Allah, Glory and Majesty be to Him, before I saw Him.[17]

He has also been quoted as saying the following, "I wish I was my family's sheep. They would have fattened me up to the maximum. When they were visited by friends, they would have killed me and roasted part of me, and made qadid (meat cut into strips and dried) from the other part of it,

then they would have eaten me, and lastly, they would have relieved me with their bowel evacuation ... I wish I had been all that, rather than a human being."[18]

Abu Bakr apparently said a similar thing to the above. He looked at a bird on a tree, and then said, "Well done bird ... you eat the fruits, you stand on the trees and you are not accountable to anybody nor indeed can anybody punish you. I wish I was a tree by the road and that a camel would come along and eat me. Then relieve me with his bowel evacuation ... I wish that I had been all that, rather than a human being."[19]

MinHajj as Sunnah, Ibn Taymiyya, vol 3 p 120 He also said, "I wish that my mother had not given birth to me ... I wish I was a straw in the mud."[20] These are some texts that I used just as examples and not for any specific reason.

And this is the Book of Allah which gives the good news to the worshippers of Allah who believe in Him:

> *"Now surely the friends of Allah, they shall have no fear, nor shall they grieve. Those who believe and fear (Allah), they shall have good news in this world's life and in the Hereafter,*

there is no changing in the words of Allah; that is the great achievement." *(Holy Qur'an 10:62-64)*

Allah also says:

"(As for) those who say, our Lord is Allah, then continue in the right way, the angels descend upon them, saying, 'Fear not, nor be grieved, and receive good news of the garden which you were promised. We are your guardians in this world's life and in the Hereafter, and you shall have therein what your souls desire and you shall have therein what you ask for. An entertainment by the Forgiving, the Merciful.' (Holy Our'an 41:30-32)

How could the two Shaykhs, Abu Bakr and Umar, wish that they were not from the human race, which Allah honored and put it above all His creation? Even the ordinary believer, who keeps on the straight path during his lifetime, receives the angels to tell him about his place in heaven, and that he should not fear the torture of Allah, nor be depressed about his legacy in life, and that he has the good news while he is in this life before reaching the life Hereafter.

Then how could the great Companions, who are the best of creation after the Messenger of Allah (so we have been taught), wish they were excrement or a hair or a straw when the angels had given them the good news that they would go to heaven? They could not have wished to have all the gold on earth to ransom themselves from the torture of Allah before meeting Him.

Allah, the Most High, said:

"And if every soul that has done injustice had all that is in the earth, it would offer it for ransom, and they will

manifestly regret when they see the chastisement and the matter shall be decided between them with justice and they shall not be dealt unjustly." (Holy Quran 10:54)

Allah also said:

"And had those who are unjust all that is in the earth and the like of with it, they would certainly offer it as ransom (to be saved) from the evil of the punishment on the day of resurrection; and what they never thought of shall become plain to them from Allah. And the evil (consequences) of what they wrought shall become plain to them, and the very thing they mocked at shall beset them." (Holy Qur'an 39:47-48)

I wish sincerely that these Qur'anic verses did not involve great companions like Abu Bakr al-Siddiq and Umar al-Faruq. But I often pause when I read these texts so that I can look at some interesting aspects of their relations with the Messenger of Allah (saw), and how that relation went through much turmoil.

They disobeyed his orders and refused him his wishes, even in the last moments of his blessed and honorable life, which made him so angry that he ordered them all to leave his house and to leave him. I also recall the chain of events that took place after the death of the Messenger of Allah, and the hurt and lack of recognition that afflicted his daughter al-Zahra. The Messenger of Allah (saw) said, "Fatimah is part of me, he who angers her angers me."[21]

Fatimah said to Abu Bakr and Umar: "I ask you in the name of Allah, the Most High, did you not hear the Messenger of Allah (saw) saying, 'The satisfaction of Fatimah is my satisfaction, and the anger of Fatimah is my anger, he who loves my daughter Fatimah loves me, and he who satisfies Fatimah satisfies me, and he who angers Fatimah angers me?' They said, 'Yes, we heard it from the Messenger of Allah (saw).' Then she said, 'Therefore, I testify before Allah and the angels that you have angered me and did not please me, and if I meet the Prophet I will complain to him about you.'[22]

Let us leave this tragic story for the time being, but Ibn Qutaybah, who is considered to be one of the great Sunni scholars, and was an expert in many disciplines and wrote many books on Qur'anic commentary. Hadith Linguistics, grammar and history might well have been converted to Shiism, as somebody I know once claimed when I showed him Ibn Qutaybah's book "History of the Caliphs."

This is the type of propaganda that some of our scholars use when they lose the argument. Similarly al-Tabari was a Shi'ite, and al-Nisa'i, who wrote a book about the various aspects of Imam 'Ali, was a Shiite, and Taha Husayn, a contemporary scholar who wrote "Al-Fitnah al-Kubra" and other facts, was also a Shi'ite!

The fact is that all of these were not Shiites, and when they talked about the Shi'a, they said all sorts of dishonorable things about them, and they defended the fairness of the Companions with all their might. But the fact is that whenever a person mentions the virtues of 'Ali ibn Abi Talib, and admits to the mistakes that were committed by the famous Companions; we say that he has become a Shiite.

And if you say in front of them, when you mention the Prophet, "May Allah bless him and his Family" or say, "'Ali, may Allah's peace be upon him" then you are branded a Shiite. According to that premise, one day, during a debate, I asked one of our scholars, "What do you think of al- Bukhari?"

He said, "He is one of the leading authorities in Hadith (the Prophetic tradition) and we consider his book to be the most correct book after the

Book of Allah, as all our scholars agree." I said to him, "He is a Shiite."

He laughed and said, "God forbid that Imam al-Bukhari be a Shiite." I said, "Did you not say that whoever says 'Ali, may Allah's peace be upon him, is Shiite?" He answered, "Yes." Then I showed him and those who were with him al-Bukhari's book, and in many places when 'Ali's name appears, he put "May Allah's peace be upon him" as well as the names of Fatimah and al- Husayn. The man did not know what to say.[23]

Let us return to the incident mentioned by Ibn Qutaybah in which Fatimah allegedly was angered by Abu Bakr and Umar. If I doubt the authenticity of that story, then I could not doubt the authenticity of al-Bukhari's book, which we consider to be the most correct book after the Book of Allah. As we have committed ourselves to the fact that it is correct, then the Shiites have the right to use it in their protestation against us and force us to keep to our commitment, as is only fair for sensible people.

In his book, al-Bukhari writes in a chapter entitled "The virtues of the relatives of the Messenger of Allah" the following: The Messenger of Allah (saw) said, "Fatimah is part of me, and whoever angers her angers me." Also in a chapter about "The Khaybar Raid" he wrote: According to Aishah, Fatimah- may Allah's peace be upon her - daughter of the Prophet, sent a message to Abu Bakr asking him for her share of the inheritance of the Messenger of Allah, but he refused to pay Fatimah anything of it. Fatimah became so angry at Abu Bakr that she left him and never spoke to him before her death.[24]

The final result is one, al-Bukhari mentioned it briefly and Ibn Qutaybah talked about it in some detail, and that is: the Messenger of Allah (saw) is angry when Fatimah is angry, and he is satisfied when Fatimah is satisfied, and that she died while she was still angry with Abu Bakr and Umar.

If al-Bukhari said: She died while she was still angry at Abu Bakr, and did not speak to him before she died, then the end result is quite clear. If Fatimah is "the leading lady among all the ladies" as al-Bukhari declared in the section al-Isti'dhan, and if Fatimah is the only lady in this nation whom Allah kept clean and pure, then her anger could not be but just, therefore Allah and His Messenger get angry for her anger. Because of that Abu Bakr said, "May Allah, the Most High, save me from His anger and Fatimah's anger." Then he cried very bitterly when she said, "By Allah, I will curse you in every prayer that I do." He came out crying and said, "I do not need your pledge of allegiance and discharge me from my duties."[25]

Many of our historians and scholars admit that Fatimah, may Allah's peace be upon her, challenged Abu Bakr in many cases such as the donations, the inheritance and the shares of the relatives, but her challenge was dismissed, and she died angry at him. However, our scholars seem to pass over these incidents without having the will to talk about them in some detail, so that they could as usual, preserve the integrity of Abu Bakr. One of the strange things that I have read regarding this subject, is what one of the writers said after he had mentioned the incident in some detail: God forbid that Fatimah should claim something that does not rightly belong to her, and God forbid that Abu Bakr denied her rights.

The writer thought that through this weak reasoning, he would be able to solve the problem and convince the researchers. He appears to be saying something similar to the following: God forbid that the Holy Qur'an should say anything but the truth, and God forbid that the sons of Israel should worship the calf. We have been plagued with scholars who say things that they cannot comprehend, and believe in the object and its antithesis, simultaneously. The point is that Fatimah claimed and Abu Bakr dismissed her claim, so she was either a liar - God forbid - or Abu Bakr treated her unjustly. There could be no third solution for the case, as some of our scholars would wish.

Logical reasoning and traditional proofs prevent the Mistress of Ladies from being accused of lying, due to the confirmation of her father (s) in his saying: "Fatimah is a part of me, and whoever hurts her hurts me." Hence, intuitively, whoever lies does not deserve this kind of statement (of honor) by the Messenger of Allah (saw). Therefore, the saying itself is a clear indication of her infallibility.

The purification verse from the Holy Qur'an is another indication of her infallibility, and it was revealed in her honor and the honor of her husband and her two sons, as Aishah herself testified.[26] Hence, there is nothing left for sensible people but to accept the fact that she was unjustly treated, and that she was easy to be branded a liar by somebody who was willing to let her burn unless the remaining people in her house came out to vote for him.[27]

Because of that, she, may Allah's peace be upon her, refused entry to Abu Bakr and Umar when they asked her permission. Even when 'Ali allowed them to enter, she turned her face to the wall and refused to look at them.[28] Furthermore, before she died, she asked to be buried secretly, and at night, so that none of them could be present at her funeral,[29] and to this day, the grave of the Prophet's daughter is unknown.

I would like to ask why our scholars remain silent about these facts, and are reluctant to look into them, or even to mention them. They give us the impression that the Companions are like angels, infallible and sinless, and when you ask them why the caliph of the Muslim's Uthman was murdered, they would say: It was the Egyptians, and they were not believers who came and killed him thus ends the subject with two words.

When I had the opportunity to carry out research into history, I found that the main figures behind the killing of Uthman were the Companions themselves, and that Aishah led them, calling for his death publicly and saying: "Kill Na'thal (the old fool), for he was not a believer."[30]

Also we know that Talhah, al-Zubayr, Muhammad ibn Abi Bakr and other famous Companions besieged him in his house and prevented him from having a drink of water, so that they could force him to resign. Furthermore, the historians inform us that they did not allow his corpse to be buried in a Muslim cemetery, and that he was finally buried in "Hashsh Kawkab" without washing the corpse and without a shroud.

O Allah, praise be to You, how could they tell us that he was unjustly killed, and that those who killed him were not Muslims. This is another case similar to that of Fatimah and Abu Bakr: Uthman was either unjustly treated, therefore we may pass judgment on those Companions who killed him or those who participated in his killing that they were criminal murderers because they unlawfully killed the caliph of the Muslims, and threw stones at his funeral, and humiliated him when he was alive and then when he was dead; or that the Companions killed him because he committed certain deeds which were not compatible with Islam, as the historical sources tell us.

There is no third option, unless we dismiss the historical facts and accept the distorted picture that the Egyptians, who were not believers, killed Uthman. In both cases there is a definite rejection of the common belief that all the Companions were right and just, without exception, for either Uthman was unjust or his killers were not just, but all of them were Companions, and hence our proposition becomes void. Therefore we are left with the proposition of the followers of Ahl al-Bayt, and that is that some of the Companions were right and some others were wrong.

We may ask a few questions about the war of al-Jamal, which was instigated by Umm al-Mumineen Aishah, who played an important role in it. How could Umm al-Mumineen Aishah leave her house in which Allah had ordered her to stay, when the most High said:

"And stay in your houses and do not display your finery

like the displaying of the ignorance of yours." (Holy Qur'an 33:33)

We may also ask, how could Aishah allow herself to declare war on the caliph of the Muslims, 'Ali ibn Abi Talib, who was the master of all Muslims? As usual, our scholars, with some simplicity, answer us that she did not like Imam 'Ali because he advised the Messenger of Allah to divorce her in the incident of al-Ifk. Seemingly these people are trying to convince us that that incident - if it was true - namely 'Ali's advice to the Prophet to divorce Aishah, was sufficient for her to disobey the orders of her God and her husband, the Messenger of Allah.

She rode a camel that the Messenger of Allah forbade her from riding and warned her about the barking of al-Hawab's dogs,[31] she travelled long distances from al-Medinah to Mekka then to Basrah, she permitted the killing of innocent people and started a war against the commander of the believers and the Companions who voted for him, and she caused the deaths of thousands of Muslims, according to the historians.[32] She did all that because she did not like 'Ali who advised the Prophet to divorce her.

Nevertheless the Prophet did not divorce her so why all this hatred towards Imam 'Ali? History has recorded some aggressive stances against 'Ali that could not be explained and these are some of them. When she was on her way back from Mekka Aishah was informed that Uthman was killed, so she was delighted, but when she learnt that people had voted for 'Ali to succeed him she became very angry and said, "I wish the sky would collapse on the earth before Ibn Abi Talib succeeds to the caliphate." Then she said, "Take me back." Thus she started the civil war against 'Ali, whose name she never liked to mention, as many historians agree.

Had Aishah heard the saying of the Messenger of Allah (saw): "Loving

'Ali is believing, and hating him is hypocrisy"?[33] To the extent that some of the Companions used to say, "We recognized the hypocrites by their hatred of 'Ali." Had Aishah not heard the saying of the Prophet: Whoever accepts me as his master, then 'Ali is his master? Undoubtedly she heard all that, but she did not like it, and she did not like mentioning his name, and when she learnt of his death she knelt and thanked Allah.[34]

Let us move on, for I do not want to discuss the life of Umm al- Mumineen Aishah, but I have tried to show how many of the Companions violated the principles of Islam and disobeyed the orders of the Messenger of Allah (saw), and it suffices to mention the following incident which happened to Aishah during the civil war, and on which all historians tend to agree.

It has been said that when Aishah passed by the waters of al-Hawab and heard the dogs barking, she remembered the warning of her husband, the Messenger of Allah, and how he prevented her from being the instigator of "al-Jamal" war. She cried, and then she said, "Take me back. Take me back!" But Talhah and al- Zubayr brought fifty men and bribed them, then made them testify that these waters were not al-Hawab's waters. Later she continued her journey until she reached Basrah. Many historians believe that those fifty men gave the first falsified testimony in the history of Islam.[35]

O Muslims! You, who have enlightened minds, assist us in solving this problem. Were these truly the honorable Companions, of whom we were always led to believe in their righteousness, and that they were the best people after the Messenger of Allah (saw)! How could they give a falsified testimony when the Messenger of Allah considered it to be one of the great sins, whose punishment is Hell?

The same question crops up again. Who was right and who was wrong? Either 'Ali and his followers were wrong, or Aishah and her followers and Talhah and al-Zubayr and their followers were wrong. There is no third possibility. But I have no doubt that the fair researcher would take 'Ali's side and dismiss Aishah and her followers who instigated the civil war that devastated the nation and left its tragic marks to the present day.

For the sake of further clarification and for the sake of my own satisfaction I mention here what al-Bukhari had to say in his book about the civil war. When Talhah, al-Zubayr and Aishah travelled to Basrah, 'Ali sent Ammar ibn Yasir and al-Hasan ibn 'Ali to al-Kufah. On their arrival, they went to the mosque and addressed the congregation, and we heard Ammar saying, "Aishah had gone to Basrah and by Allah she is the wife of your Prophet in this life and the life hereafter, but Allah, the Most High, is testing you to know whom you obey: Him or her."[36]

Also al-Bukhari wrote in his book a chapter about what went on in the houses of the Prophet's wives: Once the Prophet (saw) was giving a speech, and he indicated the house where Aishah was living, then said, "There is the trouble...there is the trouble...there is the trouble...from where the devil's horns come out ..."[37]

Al-Bukhari wrote many strange things in his book about Aishah and her bad manners towards the Prophet to the extent that her father had to beat her until she bled. He also wrote about her pretention towards the Prophet until Allah threatened her with divorce... and there are many other stories but we are limited by space.

After all that I ask how did Aishah deserve all that respect from the Sunnis; is it because she was the Prophet's wife? But he had so many wives, and some of them were better than Aishah, as the Prophet himself declared.[38]

Or perhaps because she was Abu Bakr's daughter! Or maybe because she played an important role in the denial of the Prophet's will for 'Ali, and when she was told that the Prophet recommended 'Ali, she said, "Who said that? I was with the Prophet (saw) supporting his head on my chest, then he asked me to bring the washbowl, as I bent down he died, so I cannot see how he recommended 'Ali."[39]

Or is it because she fought a total war against him and his sons after him, and even intercepted the funeral procession of al-Hasan, Leader of the Heaven's youth, and prevented his burial beside his grandfather, the Messenger of Allah, and said "Do not allow anybody that I do not like to enter my house."

She forgot, or maybe ignored the Messenger of Allah's sayings about him and his brother, "Allah loves those who love them, and Allah hates those who hate them," Or his saying, "I am at war with those who fight against you, and I am at peace with those who appease you." And there are many other sayings in their honor. No wonder, for they were so dear to him!

She heard many more sayings in honor of 'Ali, but despite the Prophet's warning, she was determined to fight him and agitate the people against him and deny all his virtues. Because of that, the Umayyads loved her and put her in a high position and filled the books with her virtues and made her the great authority for the Islamic nation because she had half of the religion.

Perhaps they assigned the second half of the religion to Abu Hurayrah, who told them what they wanted to hear, so they bestowed on him various honors: they gave him the governorship of al-Medinah, they gave him al- Aqiq palace and gave him the title of "Rawiat al-Islam", the transmitter of Islam.

He made it easy for the Umayyads to create a completely new religion which took whatever pleased them and supported their interests and power from the Holy Qur'an and the tradition of the Prophet. Inevitably, such a religion lacked any seriousness and became full of contradictions and myths; hence most of the facts were buried and replaced by lies. Then they forced the people to believe in these lies so that the religion of Allah became a mere joke, and no one feared Allah as much as they feared Muawiah.

When we ask some of our scholars about Muawiah's war against 'Ali, who had been acknowledged by al-MuHajjireen and al-Ansar, a war which led to the division of Islam into Sunnis and Shiites and left it scarred to this very day, they simply answer by saying, "'Ali and Muawiah were both good Companions, and both of them interpreted Islam in his own way. However, 'Ali was right, therefore he deserves two rewards, but Muawiah got it wrong, therefore, he deserves one reward. It is not within our right to judge for them or against them, Allah, the Most High, said:

This is a people that have passed away, they shall have what they earned and you shall have what you earn, and you shall not be called upon to answer for what they did.'" (Holy Qur'an 2:134)

Regrettably, we provide such weak answers that neither a sensible mind nor a religion, nor indeed a law would accept. O Allah, I am innocent of idle talk and of deviant whims. I beg You to protect me from the devil's touch.

How could a sensible mind accept that Muawiah had worked hard to interpret Islam and give him one reward for his war against the leader of all Muslims, and for his killing of thousands of innocent believers, in addition to all the crimes that he committed? He was known among the historians for killing his opponents through feeding them poisoned honey, and he used to say, "Allah has soldiers made of honey."

How could these people judge him as a man who worked hard to promote Islam and give him a reward for that, when he was the leader of a wrong faction? There is a well-known Hadith of the Prophet, and most of the scholars agree its authenticity, "Woe unto Ammar...he will be killed by the wrong faction." And he was killed by Muawiah and his followers.

How could they judge him as a promoter of Islam when he killed Hijr Ibn Adi and his companions and buried them in Marj Adhra in the Syrian desert because they refused to curse 'Ali ibn Abi Talib?

How could they judge him a just Companion when he killed al-Hasan, leader of the Heaven's youth, by poisoning him?

How could they judge him as being correct after he had forced the nation to acknowledge him as a caliph and to accept his corrupt son Yazid as his successor, and to change the Shurah (consultative) system to a hereditary one?[40]

How could they judge him as a man who had worked hard to promote Islam and to reward him, after he forced the people to curse 'Ali and Ahl al- Bayt, the Family of the chosen Prophet, and killed those Companions who refused to do so, and made the act of cursing 'Ali a tradition? There is no power but in Allah, the Most High, the Great.

The question crops up over and over again. Which faction was right, and which faction was wrong? Either 'Ali and his followers were wrong, or Muawiah and his followers were wrong, and the Messenger of Allah (saw) explained everything.

In both cases, the proposition of the righteousness of all the Companions does not hold ground and is incompatible with logic. There are many examples for all these subjects. and if I want to study them in detail and discuss them for all their aspects, then I would need volumes.

But I wanted to be brief in this study so I mentioned a few examples, but thank Allah, for they have been enough to refute the claims of my people who froze my mind for a period of time, and prevented me from looking at the Hadith (prophetic tradition) and the historical events with an analytical view, using the intellect and the legal yard-sticks which the Holy Qur'an and the honorable Prophet's tradition taught us to do.

153

Therefore, I shall rebel against myself and rid myself of the dust of prejudice with which they engulfed me. I shall free myself from all the chains and fetters that I have been tied with for more than twenty years, and say, "I wish my people knew that Allah has granted me forgiveness and made me among the honorable people. I wish my people could discover the world they know nothing about, but nevertheless oppose."

Notes

1. Sahih, Bukhari, vol 1 p 122 (al Idayn book)
2. al Khilafah wa al Mulk, Syed Abul A'la Maududi, p 106
3. Sahih, Muslim, vol 1 p 61
4. Sahih, Bukhari, vol 2 p 305Sahih, Muslim, vol 2 p 356, Mustadrak, al Hakim, vol 3 p 109
5. Sahih, Bukhari, vol 1 p 76, Sahih, Tirmidhi, vol 5 p 300 Sunan, Ibn Majah, vol 1 p 44
6. Sahih, Muslim, vol 1 p 61; Sunan, al Nasai, vol 6 p 117; Sahih, al Tirmidhi, vol 8 p 306
7. Sahih, Tirmidhi, vol 5 p 201; Mustadrak, al Hakim, vol 3 p 126
8. Musnad, Ahmed Hanbal, vol 5 p 25; Mustadrak, Hakim, vol 3 p 134;Sahih, al Tirmidhi, vol 5 p 296
9. Sahih, Muslim, vol 2 p 362; Mustadrak, Hakim, vol 3 p 109; Musnad, Ahmed Hanbal, vol 4 p 281
10. Mustadrak, hakim, vol 3 p 121; Khasais, al Nasai, p 24; Musnad, Ahmed Hanbal, vol 6 p 33; al Manaqib, al Khawarizmi, p 81; al Riyadh al Nadira, Tabari, vol 2 p 219; Tarikh, as Suyuti, p 73
11. Sahih, Bukhari, vol 2 p 134 12.
12. Sahih, Bukhari, vol 2 p 154; Sahih, Muslim, vol 1 p 260
13. Sahih, Muslim, vol 2 p 134
14. Sahih, Bukhari, vol 1 p 54
15. Sahih, Bukhari, vol 2 p 135

16. Sahih, Bukhari, vol 3 p 32
17. Sahih, Bukhari, vol 2 p 201
18. MinHajj as Sunnah, Ibn Taymiyya, vol 3 p 131; Hilyat al Awliya, Ibn Abi Nuaym, vol 1 p 52
19. Tarikh, Tabari, p 41; al Riyadh al Nadira, vol 1 p 134; Kanz al Ummal, p 361
20. Tarikh, Tabari, p 41; al Riyadh al Nadira, Tatabri, vol 1 p 134; Kanz al Ummal, p 361; MinHajj as Sunnah, Ibn Taymiyya, vol 3 p 120
21. Sahih, Bukhari, vol 2 p 206
22. al Imamah Was Siyasah, Ibn Qutaybah, vol 1 p 20; Muhammad Baqir as Sadr, Fadak in History, p 92
23. Sahih, Bukhari, vol 1 p 127, 130, vol 2 p 126, 205
24. Sahih, Bukhari, vol 3 p 39
25. Tarikh al Khulafa, Ibn Qutaybah, vol 1 p 20
26. Sahih, Muslim, vol 7 p 121, 130
27. Tarikh al Khulafa, vol 1 p 20
28. Tarikh al Khulafa, vol 1 p 20
29. Sahih, Bukhari, vol 3 p 39
30. Tarikh, Tabari, vol 4 p 407; Tarikh, Ibn Athir, vol 3 p 206; Lisan al Arab, vol 14 p 193; Taj al Arus, vol 8 p 141; Al Iqd al Farid, vol 4 p 290
31. al Imamah was Siyasah
32. Al Tabari, Ibn al Athir and other historians who wrote about the events in the Year 36 A.H
33. Sahih, Muslim, vol 1 p 48
34. Al Tabari, Ibn al Athir, who wrote about the events in the Year of 40 Hijri
35. Al Tabari, Ibn al Athir and other historians who wrote about the events of the Year 40 A.H
36. Sahih, Bukhari, vol 4 p 161

37. Sahih, Bukhari, vol 2 p 128
38. Sahih al Tirmidhi; al Istiab, Ibn Abd al Barr, Biography of Safiyya
39. Sahih, Bukhari, vol 3 p 68
40. Read Khilafat o Mulukiyat by Syed Abul A'la Maududi

The Beginning of the Change

I stayed unsettled and perplexed for three months, even when I was asleep; my mind was overwhelmed by doubts and fears about myself regarding the Companions whose lives I was researching. I found many astonishing contradictions in their behavior, because throughout my life I had received an education based on the respect and the veneration of those sages who would hurt anybody that spoke badly about them or disrespected them in their absence, even if they were dead.

I had read once in "Hayat al-Haywan al-Kubra" by alDamiri:[1] There was a man riding in a Caravan with his friend, and during the journey he kept insulting Umar, and his friend tried to prevent him from doing so. When he was in the toilet, a black snake bit him, and he died immediately. When they dug his grave, they found a black snake inside it; they dug another one, and the same thing happened. Every time they dug a new grave, they found a snake inside it.

Then a learned man told them, "Bury him anywhere you wish, even if you dig the whole earth, you will find a black snake. This is because Allah wants to chastise him in this life before the hereafter, for insulting our master Umar."

Thus, while I was forcing myself through this difficult research, I felt fearful and confused, especially as I had learnt in al-Zaytuna that the best caliphs were Abu Bakr al-Siddiq then Umar ibn al-Khattab al-Farooq, whom Allah will use to divide right from wrong, after that comes Uthman ibn Affan Dhul-Noorayn, from whom the angels of the Merciful felt shy, and after him comes 'Ali ibn Abi Talib the gate to the city of knowledge.

After these four come the remaining six of the ten who were promised Paradise, and they are Talhah, al-Zubayr, Sa'ad, Sa'eed, Abdul-Rahman, and Abu Ubaydah. After them come all the Companions, and after we were recommended of the Holy Qur'anic verse "We do not differentiate between any of His messengers" as a premise on which we should base the assumption that we should not differentiate in our respect for all the Companions.

Because of that I feared for myself, and asked my Lord for forgiveness on many occasions, and indeed I wanted to leave the issues that made me doubtful about the Companions of the Messenger of Allah, and then made me doubtful about my own religion.

During that period, and throughout my conversations with a few learned people, I found many contradictions that could not be accepted by sensible people, and then they started to warn me that if I continued with my research about the Companions, Allah would take His grace from me and finish me off.

Their continuous stubbornness and their denial of whatever I said, coupled with my scientific mind and eagerness to reach the truth, forced me to resume the research, because I felt an inner force urging me to do so.

Note

1. Hayat al Haywan al Kubra, al Damiri

A Dialogue With a Scholar

I said to one of our scholars: "When Muawiah killed the innocent and disgraced the honourable, you judge him as being an interpreter of Islam who got it wrong, and therefore has one reward. When Yazid killed the descendants of the Messenger and authorized the sacking of al-Medinah al- Munawwarah by his army, you judge him as an interpreter of Islam who got it wrong, and therefore has one reward.

Some of you even said about him that 'al-Husayn was killed by the sword of his grandfather.' Why should I not then interpret Islam through this study, which is forcing me to doubt the intentions of the Companions and to blow the cover of some of them, which would not be equated with killings done by Muawiah and Yazid of the Prophet's family? If I am right I deserve two rewards, and if I am wrong, I would have only one reward.

However, my criticism of the Companions is not for the sake of insulting them or cursing them, but it is a means through which I hope to reach the truth. Who is the right group, and who is the wrong group. This is my duty and the duty of each Muslim, and Allah, praise be to Him, knows what is inside ourselves. The scholar then answered me, '

O my son, Ijtihad (the interpretation of Islamic religion) has not been allowed for some time."

I asked, "Who disallowed it?" He said, "The four Imams."

I said liberally, "Thanks be to Allah! Since neither Allah disallowed it, nor His Messenger or the rightly guided caliphs, whom we are ordered to follow, then there are no restrictions on me to interpret Islam, as they did."

He said, "You may not interpret Islam unless you know seventeen disciplines, among them: Tafsir (commentary on the Holy Qur'an), Linguistics, Grammar, Sarf (Morphology), Rhetoric, Hadiths (Prophetic traditions), History and others."

I interjected by saying, "My Ijtihad is not to show the people the rules of the Qur'an and the Prophet's tradition, or to be a religious leader of a new creed. Nay! All that I want to know is who is right and who is wrong. For example, to know whether Imam 'Ali was right or Muawiah, I do not need to master seventeen disciplines. All I need to do is to study the life and works of each one of them to know the truth."

He said, "Why do you want to know all that?

This is a people that have passed away; they shall have what they earned and you shall have what you earn, and you shall not be called upon to answer for what they did." (Holy Qur'an 2:134)

I asked, "Do you read Tusaloon (the Arabic word for Questioned) with Dammah (the vowel point upon the letter ta) or with Tasaloon with Fathah (the vowel) point a)?"

He said, "Tusaloon, with Dammah."

I said, Thanks be to Allah, if it was with Fathah, then there would be no research. As it is written with Dammah, then it means that Allah

- praise be to Him - will not make us accountable for what they have done, similarly, He, the Most High, said:

> *"Each soul is pledged to whatever it has earned."* **(Holy Qur'an 74:38)**

Also He said:

> *"There is nothing for man except what he has strived for."* **(Holy Qur'an 53:39)**.

And the Holy Qur'an urged us to know about the earlier nations and to learn lessons from their histories. Also, Allah told us about the Pharaohs, Haman, Nimrod, Quaroon, and about the early prophets and their nations, not for the sake of pleasure, but to show us what is right and what is wrong. As for your question as to why I want to know all that? It is important for me to know all that.

Firstly, to know who is the friend of Allah so that I may befriend him, and to know who is the enemy of Allah, so that I may oppose him, and that is what the Qur'an asked me, or indeed, ordered me to do.

Secondly, it is important for me to know how I should worship Allah and draw near to Him by obeying His commands, in the way He - the Majesty - wants them to be, not as Malik or Abu Hanifa or any other interpreter of Islam wants them to be.

I found that Malik does not prefer the saying of "In the name of Allah the most Merciful and the most Compassionate" during the prayers, whereas Abu Hanifa considers it a "must". Others say that the prayers are not valid without them. Because prayers are a pillar of Islam, if accepted other deeds would be accepted; but if they were rejected, other deeds would be rejected. Therefore, I do not want my prayers to be invalid. The Shiites say that during the ablution we must rub our feet with wet hands, whereas the Sunnis say that we must wash them. But when we read the Holy Qur'an we find "rub your hands and feet" which is clear about the rubbing. So how do you expect any sensible Muslim to accept this and reject the other without research and analysis?"

He said, "You can take what you like from each creed, because all of them are Islamic creeds, and all of them came from the Messenger of Allah."

I said I am afraid that I may become one of those about whom Allah said:

> *"Have you then considered him who takes his low desire for his god and Allah has made him err having knowledge and has set a seal upon his ear and his heart and put a covering upon his eye. Who can then guide him after Allah? Will you not then be mindful?" (Holy Qur'an 45:23).*

Sir, I do not think that all the four Islamic religious schools (Madhahib) are correct, as long as one of them allows something while the other forbids it; and it does not seem logical for one thing to be allowed and forbidden simultaneously. The Messenger of Allah (saw) did not question the rules of the Holy Qur'an because they are revelation:

> *"And if it were from any other than Allah, they would have found in it many a discrepancy." (Holy Qur'an 4:82).*

Because of the vast differences between the four religious Islamic schools, they cannot be from Allah or from His Messenger, for the Messenger did not contradict the Holy Qur'an.

When the scholarly Shaykh found my argument logical and sound, he said, "I advise you, for the sake of Allah, that no matter how doubtful you may be, do not doubt the rightly guided caliphs, because they are the four pillars of Islam, if one of them collapses, the whole building will collapse."

I said, "God forbid Sir, but what about the Messenger of Allah if those people were the pillars of Islam?"

He said, "The Messenger of Allah is that building He is the whole of Islam."

I smiled when I heard his analysis, and said, "I ask Allah for forgiveness, yet again! Sir, you are saying, indirectly, that the Messenger of Allah (saw) would not be able to stand without the support of those four, whereas Allah, the Most High, says:

"He it is Who sent His messenger with guidance and a true religion that He may make it prevail over all the religions; and Allah is enough for a witness." (Holy Qur'an 48:28)

He sent Muhammad with the Message and did not involve any of the other four, or anybody else, and Allah said with regard to this:

"We have sent among you a messenger from among you who recites to you Our communications and purifies you and teaches you the Book and the wisdom and teaches you that which you did not know." (Holy Qur'an 2:151).

He said, "That is what we have learnt from our religious leaders and teachers, and we did not argue about what they taught us, as you the new generation do today. You doubt everything, even the religion itself. This is one sign of the nearness of the Hour, that is the Day of Judgment, and the Messenger of Allah said: the Hour will come as a result of the evil in people."

I said, "Sir, why all this exaggeration? God forbid if I doubt the religion, I believe in Allah, Who is unique and has no partner. I believe in His angels, Books and Messengers. I believe in our master Muhammad as His servant and Messenger, and that he is the best of all the prophets and the last of the messengers, and that I am one of the Muslims. So how could you accuse me of all that?"

He said, "I accuse you of more than that, because you doubt our masters Abu Bakr and Umar, and the Holy Prophet said: If the faith of my nation and the belief of Abu Bakr were put on a balance, the faith of Abu Bakr would have weighed heavier. The Holy Prophet also said in honor of Umar: 'I was shown my nation and each one of them was wearing a shirt that came to the chest, and I was shown Umar and he was pulling his shirt.' They said: 'O Messenger of Allah! How do you interpret this? He said: 'The Religion.

And you come today, in the fourteenth century (Hijri) and doubt the righteousness of the Companions and especially Abu Bakr and Umar. Don't you know that the people of Iraq are the people of disunity, blasphemy and hypocrisy!'"

What could I say to this man who claimed knowledge and scholarship, and who became so arrogant that he changed a well structured dialogue into a disordered talk full of lies and propaganda? He said it in front of people who admired him, and I noticed that their faces lit up with excitement and evil.

I quickly went home and brought back two books, "al-Muwatta of Imam Malik" and "The Sahih of al-Bukhari". Then said, "Sir, what made me doubt Abu Bakr was the Messenger of Allah himself." I opened al-Muwatta and read: He said to the martyrs of Uhud, "Those, I bear witness against." Abu Bakr then said, "O Messenger of Allah, are we not their brothers? Did we not become Muslims as they did? Did we not fight as they did?"

The Messenger replied, "Yes, but I do not know what you are going to do after me."

On hearing that, Abu Bakr cried bitterly and said, "We are going to alter many things after your departure."¹

After that I opened the "Sahih" of al-Bukhari and read: Once Umar ibn al-Khattab came to Hafsah and found with her Asma bint Umays. When he saw her, he asked, "Who is she?" Hafsah answered, "Asma bint Umays." Umar said, "Is she that Ethiopian?" Asma replied, "Yes." He said, "We emigrated (that is to say from Mecca to Medinah) before you, so we are more entitled to the Messenger of Allah than you."

She became very angry, then she said, "No, by Allah, you were with the Messenger of Allah, who fed your hungry people and advised the ignorant among you; whereas we were in a foreign land, in Abyssinia, for the sake of Allah and His Messenger, and whenever I ate or drank anything, I remembered the Messenger of Allah (saw) and we were hurt, and we were frightened. By Allah I will mention this to the Prophet without lying, adding anything or deviating from the subject."

When the Prophet came, she said, "O Prophet of Allah, Umar said such and such." He asked, "What did you say to him?" She answered, "Such and such." He said, "I am not more entitled to him than to you." He and his companions had one emigration, but you, people of the ship, had two emigrations." She said, "I found Abu Musa and the people of the ship coming to me in groups and asking me about the Hadith, very much delighted with what the Prophet (saw) had said to them."²

After having read the Hadiths, the looks on the faces of the scholarly Shaykh and that of the audience changed. They looked at each other and waited for the scholar, who was too shocked at what he had heard, to reply. All he did was to raise his eye brows, as a sign of astonishment and then said, "O my God grant me more knowledge."

I said, "If the Messenger of Allah (saw) was the first to doubt Abu Bakr, and did not bear witness against him, because the Messenger did not know what would happen after him; and if the Messenger of Allah did not approve of the preference of Umar over Asma bint Umays, but indeed preferred her to him; then it is within my right to doubt and not to have a preference for anybody until I know the truth. Evidently, these Hadiths contradict and nullify all the known Hadiths in favor of Abu Bakr and Umar, because they are more realistic than these which mention their alleged virtues."

The audience said, "How could that be?" I said, "The Messenger of Allah (saw) did not bear witness against Abu Bakr and said: 'I do not know what they will do after me!' This sounds very reasonable. History has proved that, and the Holy Qur'an and history bear witness that they did change after him.

Because of that Abu Bakr cried for he changed and angered Fatimah al- Zahra, daughter of the Messenger as we explained before, and he changed until he repented and wished that he was not a human being.

As for the Hadith: If the faith of my nation and the faith of Abu Bakr were put on balance, the faith of Abu Bakr would weigh heavier", it is invalid and implausible. It is not possible for the faith of a man, who spent forty years of his life believing in polytheism and worshipping idols, to be greater than the faith of the entire nation of Muhammad, which has many God-fearing and pious people and martyrs and Imams, who spent all their lives fighting for the sake of Allah.

How could Abu Bakr fit into this Hadith? If it was true, he would not, in later life have finished that he was not a human being. Further, if his faith was greater than the faith of the entire nation of Muhammad, Fatimah, the daughter of the Messenger of Allah and the leading lady, would not have been angry at him or asked Allah to punish him in each prayer she prayed."

The scholar did not say anything, but some of the men said, "By Allah! This Hadith made us doubtful." Then the scholar said to me, "Is that what you wanted? You have made these people doubt their religion." It sufficed me that a man from the audience replied by saying, "No, he is right, we have not read a whole book in our life, we followed you blindly and without any argument, and now it appears to us that what al-Hajj has been saying is right, and it is our duty to read and research!" Other people agreed with him, and that was a victory for truth and justice. It was not victory by force, but by logical deduction and proof. Allah says:

> *"Say, bring your proof, if you are telling the truth."* (Holy Qur'an 27:64)

That is what encouraged me to undertake the study and opened the door for me, so I entered it in the name of Allah by Allah and tracing the footsteps of the followers of the Messenger of Allah. I hope that Allah, praise be to Him, the Most High, grants me success and enlightenment, for He promised to enlighten anyone who searches for the truth, and He does not break His promises.

The study went on for three years, because I often re-read the books, right from the first page to the last.

I read "al-Muraja'at" by Imam Sharaf al-Din several times, since it opened new horizons for me and enlightened me and pleased me for the love and the fellowship of Ahl al-Bayt.

I read "al-Ghadeer" by Shaykh al-Amini three times because of the clear cut facts it contained. I also read Fadak in History" by al- Sayyid Muhammad Baqir al-Sadr and al-Saqifah" by Shaykh Muhammad Rida al- Muzaffar, which explained so many vague issues.

I read "al-Nass wal Ijtihad", the Text and the Interpretation, and became more convinced. Then I read "Abu Hurayra" by Sharaf al-Din and Shaykh al-Mudira" by Shaykh Mahmud Abu Rayyah al-Misri, and learnt that the Companions who changed after the departure of the Messenger of Allah were two types. The first changed the rule because of its power and authority. The second changed the rules by attributing false Hadiths to the Messenger of Allah.

I read "Imam al-Sadiq the four Madhhabs" by Asad Haydar and learnt about the differences between gifted knowledge and acquired knowledge. I also learnt about the differences between Allahs wisdom which He grants to whom He pleases, and the intrusion on knowledge and the belief of personal interpretation (of Islam) which kept the nation away from the spirit of Islam. I read more books by al-Sayyid Ja'far Murtada al-Amili, and al-Sayyid Murtada al-Askari, and Al Sayyid Al-Khusi,and al-Sayyid al-Tabatabai, and Shaykh Muhammad Amin Zain al-Din, and al-Fayroozabadi, and Ibn Abi al-Hadid al-Mu'tazili in his commentary on "Nahj al-Balagha", and Taha Husayn's "al-Fitna al-Kubra".

From the history books I read the following Annals written by al-Tabari, Ibn al-Athir, al-Masudi and al-Ya'qubi. And I read more, until I became convinced that the Shi'a Imamiyya were right.

Thus, with the help of Allah, I boarded Ahl al-Bayt's ship and sought their fellowship, because I found, thanks be to Allah, the alternative to the Companions, who, to the best of my knowledge, regressed and only a few of them were saved.

I exchanged them for the Imams of Ahl al-Bayt, the Prophet's Family, whom Allah cleansed and purified and made it our duty to seek their fellowship.

The Shiites are not, as some of our religious scholars claim, the Persians and the Magus whose power and glory were destroyed by Umar in al- Qadisiyyah war and that is why they hate them!

My answer to these who are ignorant is that following the creed of the Prophet's Family is not restricted to the Persians, for there are Shiites in Iraq, Hijaz, Syria, Lebanon, and all of them are Arabs. In addition to that, there are Shi'tes in Pakistan, India, Africa, America, and all of those are neither Arabs nor Persians.

If we confine ourselves to the Shiites of Iran, the issue becomes clearers because I found that the Persians believe in the leadership of the twelve Imams, all of whom were Arabs from Quraysh from Bani Hashim, the family of the Prophet (saw). If the Persians were prejudiced and hated the Arabs, as some people claim, they would have been taken Salman al-Farisi as their Imam, for he was a great Companion and respected by both Shiites and Sunnis.

On the other hand I found that most of the leading Sunni Imams were Persians, such as Abu Hanifa, al-Nisa'i, al-Tirmidhi, al-Bukhari, Muslim, Ibn Maja, al-Ghazali, Ibn Sina, al-Farabi and many others. If the Shiites were all Persians who rejected Umar ibn al-Khattab because he destroyed their power, then how can we explain the rejection of the Arabs who were not Persians?

Therefore, this is an illogical claim. These people refused Umar because of his role in excluding the Commander of the Believers, 'Ali ibn Abi Talib, from the caliphate after the departure of the Messenger of Allah, and because of the tragic civil wars and decline of this nation. It is high time that the truth was unveiled to every free-thinking scholar so that he may refute the allegation without any prior animosity.

It is true that the Shiites, whether they were Arabs or Persians or any other nationality, followed closely the Qur'anic Texts and the tradition of the Messenger of Allah and his Family, and refused to accept the alternative despite the oppressive policies of the Umayyads and later the Abbasids for seven centuries.

During that period, they pursued the Shiites everywhere; they killed them, they made them homeless, they denied them their rightful grants, they removed their cultural and intellectual heritage and they spread all sorts of rumors about them in order to keep people away from them. The legacy of these policies is still felt up to the present day.

However, the Shiites stood their ground, remained patient and took the blame for their commitment to Allah and they are paying the price of their defiance to this very day. I challenge any of our religious scholars to enter a debate with their religious scholars without coming out of it overwhelmed by their enlightened way.

Yes, I found the alternative, and thanks be to Allah Who guided me to this because I would not he there without His Guidance. Thanks and praise be to Allah Who led me to the saved group, for which I was eagerly searching.

I have no doubt that the commitment to 'Ali and Ahl al-Bayt is the commitment to the unbroken link - the link to Allah. There are many sayings by the Messenger of Allah agreed by all Muslims, which bear witness to that. The sensible mind is, perhaps, the best proof for anybody who is prepared to listen. 'Ali was the most knowledgeable companion and certainly the bravest, as the entire nation testified. This is a sufficient condition to support the lawful claim of 'Ali, alone and no one else, to the succession of the caliphate.

Allah the Most High said:

> *'And their prophet said to them, "Surely Allah has raised Talut to be a king over you." They said, "How can he hold kingship over us while we have a greater right to kingship than him, and he has not been granted an abundance of wealth?" He said, "Surely Allah has chosen him in preference to you, and He has increased him abundantly in knowledge and physique, and Allah grants His kingdom to whom He pleases, and Allah is Ample giving, knowing."*
> *(Holy Qur'an 2:247)*

And the Messenger of Allah said. "'Ali is from me, and I am from 'Ali, and he is the master of every believer after me."[3]

Al-Zamakhshari said in some of his poetry:

Doubt and differences have increased. Every one claims that he is the right way. But I have committed myself to: there is no other god but Allah, and my love to Ahmed (Muhammad) and 'Ali. A dog won the love of the companions of the cave, how could I be ever distressed with the love of the Prophet's Family.

Yes I found the alternative, praise be to Allah. and I became a follower of - after the Messenger of Allah - The Commander of the Believers, master of all guardians, leader of the chosen elite, the victorious lion of Allah Imam 'Ali ibn Abi Talib; and the two masters of Heaven's youth, and the Prophet's two followers, Imam Abu Muhammad al-Hasan al-Zaki, and Imam Abu Abdullah al-Husayn; and the daughter of al-Mustafa (Muhammad), mother of the Imams, the essence of the Message, she, for whom Allah feels angry if she is angered, the most honorable lady Fatimah al-Zahra.

I have changed Imam Malik for the leader of all Imams, and teacher of the nation, Imam Ja'far al-Sadiq.

I have committed myself to the nine infallible men from the posterity of al-Husayn, Imams of all Muslims and the good friends of Allah. I have changed the Companions who turned back on their heels, like Muawiah, Amr ibn al-As, al-Mughira ibn Shu'ba, Abu Hurayra, Ikrima, Ka'b al-Ahbar and others, for the grateful Companions who never broke the promise they gave to the Prophet, like Ammar ibn Yasir, Salman al-Farisi, Abu Dharr al- Ghifari, al-Miqdad ibn al-Aswad. Khuzayma ibn Thabit - Dhu al- Shahadetain - and others, and praise be to Allah for this enlightenment.

I have changed the religious leaders of my people, who discouraged us from thinking and whose majority followed the rules and the sultans, throughout time. I changed them for the devoted religious leaders of the Shi'a who never closed the opportunity for studying and interpreting Islam, and who neither rose to oppose nor submitted to the oppressive rulers.

Yes, I changed dogmatic beliefs, full of contradictions for new enlightened and liberal ones based on logical deductions and reasoning. As they say now a days "I have washed my brain" of the dirt that had accumulated over thirty years; lies of the Umayyads. I purified it with the ideology of the infallibles, those whom Allah cleansed and purified. I have done that for the remainder of my life.

O Allah...please let us live our lives following their footsteps, and let our nation follow their tradition, and gather us with them, for Your Prophet (saw) said: Man is placed together with those whom he loves.

Thus I have returned to my origin. For my father and uncles used to talk to us about our family tree. and often told us that we were from al-Sada (plural of Sayyid: a descendant of the Prophet) who escaped from Iraq under Abbasid pressure and found refuge in North Africa until they settled in Tunisia where their marks remain up to the present day.

There are many people like us in North Africa who are descendants from the purified posterity, and are called "Sada", but they went astray through the oppression of the Umayyads and the Abbasids, and now they have nothing of the truth except the people's respect for them. Priase be to Allah for his guidance...and praise be to Allah for my enlightenment and for opening my eyes to see the truth.

Notes

1. Muwatta, Malik, vol 1 p 307 ; Maghazi, al Qawidi, p 310
2. Sahih, Bukhari, vol 3 p 307
3. Sahih, al Tirmidhi, vol 5 p 296; Khasai's, al Nisai, p 87; Mustadrak, al Hakim, vol 3 p 110

The Reasons Behind the Enlightment

The reasons behind my enlightenment are many, but I shall only mention a few of them here:

The text regarding the succession to the Caliphate

I have committed myself, before embarking on this study, to never depending on any reference unless it is considered authentic by the two parties, and to discarding those references that are solely referred to by only one of the parties.

Thus, I shall investigate the idea regarding the preference between Abu Bakr and 'Ali ibn Abi Talib, and that the succession of the caliphate was by written text (Dictate) for 'Ali, as the Shiites claim, and not by election and Shura (consultation) as the Sunnis claim.

Any researcher in this subject, if he considers nothing but the truth, will find that the text in support of 'Ali is very clear, like the following saying by the Messenger of Allah: Whoever considers me his master, then 'Ali is his master. He said it at the end of the Farewell Pilgrimage, when it was confirmed that 'Ali would succeed, and many people congratulated him on that, including Abu Bakr and Umar who were among the well-wishers, and who were quoted as having said to the Imam, Well done, Ibn Abi Talib, overnight you have become a master of all the believers."¹

This text has been agreed on by both Shiites and Sunnis, and in fact I have only referred in this study to some Sunni references and not to all of them, for they are so many.

If the reader wants more information, he may read "al-Ghadir" by al- Amini (thirteen Volumes) in which the writer classifies the sayings of the Prophet according to the Sunnis.

As for the alleged popular election of Abu Bakr on "The Day of al-Saqifah" and his subsequent acclamation in the mosque; it seems that it was just an allegation without foundation. How could it be by popular agreement when so many people were absent during the acclamation? People like: 'Ali, al-Abbas, most of the house of Bani Hashim, Usama ibn Zayd, al-Zubayr, Salman al-Farisi, Abu Dharr al-Ghifari, al-Miqdad ibn al-Aswad, Ammar ibn Yasir, Hudhayfa ibn al-Yaman, Khuzayma ibn Thabit, Abu Burayd al- Aslami, al-Bura ibn Azib, Abu Ka'b, Sahl ibn Hanif, Saad ibn Ubada, Qays ibn Saad, Abu Ayyub al-Ansari, Jabir ibn Saad, Khalid ibn Saad, and many others.²

So where was the alleged popular agreement? The absence of 'Ali alone from the acclamation is sufficient to criticize that meeting because he was the only candidate for the caliphate, nominated by the Messenger of Allah, on the assumption that there was no direct text regarding such a nomination. The acclamation of Abu Bakr was without consultation; in fact it took the people by surprise, especially when the men in charge of the Muslim affairs were busy preparing for the funeral of the Messenger of Allah. The citizens of al-Medinah were shocked by the death of their Prophet, and then they forced the acclamation³ on the people, and even threatened to burn the house of Fatima if those who were absent from the acclamation refused to leave it. So how could we say that the acclamation was implemented through consultation and popular agreement?

Umar ibn al-Khattab himself testified that that acclamation was a mistake

- may Allah protect the Muslims from its evil -, and that whoever repeated it should be killed, or he might have said that if someone called for a similar action there would be no acclamation for him or for those who acclaimed him.[4]

Imam 'Ali said about that acclamation: By Allah, Ibn Abi Quhafa has got it! And he knows that my position (regarding the caliphate) is like that of the pole in relation to the millstone! The torrent flows from me, and the bird will never reach me![5]

Saad ibn Ubada, a prominent man from al-Ansar, attacked Abu Bakr and Umar on the day of "al-Saqifah," and tried hard to keep them away from the caliphate, but could not sustain his efforts, for he was ill and unable to stand, and after al-Ansar paid homage to Abu Bakr, Saad said: "By Allah I shall never pay homage to you until I cast my last arrow at you, and pierce you with my lance, and attack you with my sword, with all the power in my hand, and fight you with all the members of my family and clan.

By Allah, even if all the Jinns (invisible beings) and the human beings gathered to support you, I will never acclaim you, until I meet my God." He never prayed with them, he never sat in their company, he never performed the pilgrimage with them, and if he found a group of people willing to fight them, he would give them all his support, and if somebody acclaimed him to fight them, he would have fought them. He remained thus until he died in Syria during the caliphate of Umar.[6]

If that was a mistake (may Allah protect the Muslims from its evil) as Umar put it (and he was one of its architects, and knew what happened to the Muslims as a result of it), and if that succession to the caliphate was illegal (as Imam 'Ali described it when he said that he was the lawful nominee for it), and if that acclamation was unjust (as according to Saad ibn Ubada the leader of al-Ansar who left al-Jamaah because of it), and if that acclamation was unlawful due to the absence of the leading figures of the Companions, including al-Abbas, the uncle of the Prophet, so what is the evidence and proof which supports the legality of the Abu Bakr's succession to the caliphate?

The answer is that there is no evidence or proof with the Sunnis and al- Jamaah.

Therefore, what the Shiites say regarding this issue is right, because it has been established that the Sunnis have the text which proves the succession of 'Ali to the caliphate, but they deliberately misinterpret it to maintain the Companion's honor. Thus, the just and fair person has no choice but to accept the text, especially if he knows the circumstances that surrounded the case.[7]

The disagreement between Fatimah and Abu Bakr

The subject is agreed upon by the two parties, and the fair and sensible person has no choice but to judge Abu Bakr as being wrong, that is if he did not admit his injustice and bad treatment of the leading lady.

Anyone who cares to follow the events of that tragedy and studies its various facts will recognize that Abu Bakr deliberately hurt al-Zahra and denied her argument so that she could not protest against him - supported by the texts of al-Ghadir and others - regarding the lawful right for her husband and cousin to the succession of the caliphate. There are many indications that have been mentioned by historians which lead us to believe in accounts of these events, this is one of them:

Al-Zahra, may Allah's peace be upon her, went around the meeting places of al-Ansar, asking for support for her cousin and husband and they said, "O daughter of the Messenger of Allah, we have already acclaimed that man, and if your husband and cousin had approached us before him, we would have supported him." 'Ali, may Allah honor his face, said, "Would I leave the Messenger of Allah (saw) in his house unburied and go to argue with people about his authority?" Fatimah said, "Abu al-Hasan did what was expected from him, and for what they did Allah will hold them responsible and accountable."[8]

If Abu Bakr was wrong, either unintentionally or through goodwill, Fatimah al-Zahara would have persuaded him; but she was angry with him, because he refused to accept her argument and rejected her testimony and the testimony of her husband. She became so angry; she even prevented him in her will from being present at her funeral. When she died, her husband buried her secretly during the night.[9]

As for her secret burial (as) during the night, it is worth mentioning here, that during my years of research and investigation, I went to al-Medinah to check for myself certain points, then I discovered the following:

Firstly, the grave of al-Zahra is unknown and nobody knows exactly where it is; some say it is in the Prophet's chamber, others say it is in her house opposite the Prophet's chamber, and there are people who think that it might be in al-Baqi', in the midst of Ahl al-Bayt's graves.

This is the first fact that I deduced: al-Zahra (as) wanted the Muslims, through generations to come, to know why she asked her husband to bury her secretly during the night, and that not one of them attend her funeral! Thus, every Muslim could reach certain interesting facts when researching into historical events.

Secondly, I discovered that the visitor who wants to visit Uthman ibn Affan's grave has to go a long way until he reaches the end of al-Baqi', and there he finds it by a wall. By contrast, he will find the burial places of most of the Companions at the beginning of al-Baqi', near the entry. Even Malik ibn Anas, the famous jurist, who was a follower of the Followers, is buried near the burial places of the Messenger's wives.

It became clear to me what the historians meant when they said that he was buried in "Hash Kawkab" which was Jewish land, because the Muslims refused to bury him in the Baqi' of the Messenger of Allah. When Muawiya seized power, he bought that land from the Jews and included it in al-Baqi', so that it contains the grave of his cousin Uthman. He who visits al-Baqi' today will see this fact very clearly.

It is astonishing to know that Fatimah al-Zahra (as) was the first of the Prophet's children to die after him, and at the most there were six months between the departure of the father and his daughter, and despite that, she was not buried beside her father.

Fatimah al-Zahra, as I mentioned earlier, stated in her will that she should be buried secretly; therefore, she was not buried beside her father. But what about her son, al-Hasan, why was he not buried beside his grandfather? Aisha (Umm al-Mumineen) prevented that. When al-Husayn brought his brother to bury him by his grandfather, the Messenger of Allah, Aisha rode a mule and went around saying, "Do not bury someone I do not love in my house."

Then, the houses of Bani Umayya and Hashim stood opposite each other ready to fight, but al-Husayn told her that he would only take the coffin of his brother around the grave of their grandfather then he would bury him in al-Baqi'. That was because Imam al-Hasan requested from his brother, that no blood should be shed for his sake. Ibn Abbas said a few verses regarding this event:

"She rode a camel,[10] she rode a mule,[11] if she had lived longer, she would have ridden an elephant, you have the ninth of the eighth, and you took everything."

This is another interesting fact: How could Aisha inherit everything, when the Prophet had nine wives? Ibn Abbas transmitted to us: If the Prophet was not to leave any inheritance, and Abu Bakr bore witness to that and prevented al-Zahra from inheriting anything from her father, how then could Aisha? Is there any text which states that the wife could inherit, but not the daughter? Or was it perhaps politics that changed everything, so it denied the daughter everything, and gave the wife everything?

It is worth mentioning here a story related to the subject of inheritance that has been cited by many historians:

Ibn Abi al-Hadid al-Mutazili said in his commentary on Nahj al-Balagha: "Aisha and Hafsa came to see Uthman, during his caliphate, and asked him to give them their shares of what they had inherited from the Messenger of Allah (saw). Uthman was stretched on the sofa, so he sat up and said to Aisha: You and that woman sitting next to you brought a man who cleansed himself with his urine and testified that the Messenger of Allah (saw) said, "We, the prophets, do not leave an inheritance." If the Prophet truly did not leave any inheritance, why do you ask for it now, and if he left an inheritance, why did you deprive Fatimah of her legal share? After that, she left him feeling very angry and said: Kill Na'thal, for he has become an unbeliever."[12]

'Ali was more entitled to the leadership

One of the reasons which led to my enlightenment and ultimately made me leave the tradition (Sunna) of my forefathers was the comparison between the positions of 'Ali ibn Abi Talib and that of Abu Bakr, based on logical deductions and historical references.

As I started in earlier parts of this book, I only included in my research the references which have been agreed on by both, the Shiites and the Sunnis.

I searched in the books of both parties and found that only 'Ali received total support, and both Shiites and Sunnis agreed on his leadership in accordance with the texts they approved of. However there is neither support nor agreement on the leadership of Abu Bakr except by a small group of Muslims, and we have mentioned what Umar said about his succession to the caliphate.

Furthermore, there are many virtues and good deeds attributed to 'Ali ibn Abi Talib by the Shiites and cited as authentic references in the Sunni books. The sayings are full of the virtues of 'Ali, more than any other Companion ever received, and even Ahmed ibn Hanbal said: "No one among the Companions of the Messenger of Allah (saw) had more virtues than 'Ali ibn Abi Talib."[13]

Qadi Ismail, al-Nasa'i and Abu 'Ali al-Naisaburi said: "No Companion had as many virtues attributed to him as 'Ali."[14]

We notice that the Umayyads tried hard to force people to curse him and insult him and not to mention any of his virtues, and even they prevented anybody from being named after him, but despite all that hatred, his virtues and good deeds (as) continued to spread.

Regarding that Imam al-Shafi'i says: "I am surprised about a man, whose virtues were kept secret by his enemies, out of envy, and were kept secret by his followers, out of fear, but nevertheless, an enormous amount of them spread."

As for Abu Bakr, I searched in the books of the two parties, and found that the virtues attributed to him by the Sunnis were much less than that attributed to 'Ali. The virtues of Abu Bakr that have been mentioned in historical books were narrated either by his daughter Aisha, whose position vies-a-vies 'Ali is well documented, and she tried hard to support her father, even by fabricating sayings, or by Abdullah ibn Umar, who was never close to 'Ali, and he was one of those who refused to pay homage to 'Ali despite the popular support he had received. Abdullah ibn Umar used to say that the best people after the Prophet were Abu Bakr then Uthman, and after that everybody was equal.[15] Thus, he made Imam 'Ali like any other ordinary person, without preferences or virtues.

What was Abdullah ibn Umar's attitude towards the facts that had been mentioned by the leading personalities of the nation that "No companion had as many virtues attributed to him as 'Ali". Had Abdullah ibn Umar not heard about even one of 'Ali's virtues? Yes, by Allah, he had heard and understood, but political intrigues tend to distort the facts.

The virtues of Abu Bakr were also mentioned by Amr ibn al-'As, Abu Hurayrah, Urwa and Ikrima, and all of them hated 'Ali and fought him either with arms or by plotting against him and attributing virtues to his enemies.

Ahmed ibn Hanbal said, "'Ali had many enemies who searched hard to find a fault attributable to him, but they could not, so they brought a man whom 'Ali had-fought and battled with, and praised him because of their hatred towards 'Ali.".[16] But Allah said:

"Surely they will make a scheme, and I too will make a scheme so glad the unbelievers a respite: let them alone for a while." (Holy Qur'an 86:15- 17)

It is a miracle from Allah, praise be to Him, that the virtues of Imam 'Ali spread after six centuries of oppression and injustice against him and Ahl al- Bayt, and the Abbasids were not less evil than their predecessor the Umayyads in their treatment of Ahl al-Bayt. The poet Abu Firas al-Hamdani wrote the following verses:

"What Banu Harb have done to them is nothing in comparison to what you did to them,

How many times have you clearly violated the Religion?

And how much of the Prophet's (family's) blood has been spilt by you?

You pretend to be his followers, but on your hands is the blood of his purified sons."

After having finished with all these sayings, and having came out from the darkness, I leave the last judgment to Allah, and there will be no more excuses from the people after all that.

Despite the fact that Abu Bakr was the first caliph, and had all the power and authority, despite the bribes and gifts that the Umayyads gave to everyone who praised Abu Bakr, Umar and Uthman, and despite all the alleged virtues and good deeds that they invented for Abu Bakr, which filled many books ... despite all that, they did not amount to a fraction of the true virtues of Imam 'Ali.

Furthermore, if we analyze the alleged sayings that were in favor of Abu Bakr, we find them incompatible with the historical facts, and no sensible man or creed could accept them. Earlier on we explained the saying attributed to the Prophet: "If the faith of Abu Bakr and the faith of my nation is put on the balance, the faith of Abu Bakr will be heavier."

If the Messenger of Allah was aware of this high degree of faith in Abu Bakr, he would not have appointed Usama to command the army; nor would he have refused to bear witness for him as he did for the martyrs of Uhud, and then said to him that he did not know what he was going to do after him", so that Abu Bakr[17] cried. In addition to that, the Prophet would not have sent 'Ali ibn Abi Talib to take "Surat Bara'a" from him and prevented him from transmitting it.[18]

Nor would the Prophet have said in Khayber while presenting the flag: "Tomorrow I will give my flag to a man who loves Allah and His Messenger, ever going forward and never retreating, Allah had tested his heart with the faith", then he gave it to 'Ali and no one else.[19]

If Allah knew that Abu Bakr had such a high degree of faith, and that his faith exceeded the faith of all Muslims, Allah, praise be upon Him, would not have had to threaten him that He would spoil his work when he raised his voice above the Prophet's voice.[20]

If 'Ali and the Companions who followed him knew that Abu Bakr had this high degree of faith, they would not have hesitated to pay homage to him. If Fatimah al-Zahra, the leading lady, knew that Abu Bakr had this high degree of faith, she would not have been angry with him, nor would she have refused to talk to him or return his greetings, or cursed him in her prayers,[21] and even banned him - according to her will - from attending her funeral.

He who had such a degree of faith, and whose faith was greater than the faith of all Muslims would not have regretted, in the last moments of his life, his attitude towards Fatimah, and his burning of al-Fuja'ah al-Salami and his succession to the caliphate.[22] Also, he would not have wished not to be a human being but to be a hair or animal droppings. Is this man's faith equal to, or even greater than the faith of the entire Islamic nation?

Let us consider the saying: "If I was taking a close companion, I would have chosen Abu Bakr." This saying is like the previous one. "Where was Abu Bakr on the day of the small Brotherhood" in Mecca before the Hijra, and on the day of the great Brotherhood in Medinah after the Hijra; when in both of them the Messenger of Allah (saw) chose 'Ali as his brother then said to him, You are my brother in this life and in the Hereafter"[23] and did not turn to Abu Bakr, thus depriving him of the brotherhood in the Hereafter and from the close companionship. I do not wish to go on about this subject, and it is sufficient to bring the above mentioned examples which I have found in the Sunni books. As for the Shiites, they do not recognize these sayings at all, and they have their own clear proof that they were invented sometime after the death of Abu Bakr.

If we leave the virtues aside and concentrate on the sins, we will never find a single sin committed by 'Ali that has been mentioned in historical books (both Shiite and Sunni), whereas we find that many other people have committed sins and were mentioned in the Sunni books such as al-Sihah, the various books Sirah and annals.

Thus, we find total agreement from both parties regarding 'Ali alone, also historical facts point out that the correct acclamation was for 'Ali alone. He abstained, but the MuHajjireen and Ansar insisted on his acclamation; then when he was finally nominated, some people refused to pay homage to him, but he never forced them to change their minds.

On the other hand we find that the acclamation of Abu Bakr was a "mistake", as Umar ibn al-Khattab put it, "may Allah protect the Muslims from its evil." The acclamation of Umar was based on a promise given to him by Abu Bakr. The acclamation of Uthman was a historical comedy: Umar nominated six people for the caliphate and told them to choose one candidate, and said if four agreed and two disagreed, then the two should be killed, however, if the six were divided into two equal camps, then the camp which was supported by Abdul Rahman ibn Awf should be considered but if after a certain time passed and no agreement had been reached, the whole six should be killed.

The story is long and rather strange, but the important thing is that Abdul Rahman ibn Awf chose 'Ali on the condition that he should rule in accordance with the Book of Allah (the Qur'an) and the tradition of His Messenger and the tradition of the two Shaykhs: Abu Bakr and Umar. 'Ali refused these conditions but Uthman accepted them, so he became caliph. 'Ali came out from the conference of the acclamation and knew in advance the result, and talked about it in his famous speech known as al- Shaqshaqiyya.

After 'Ali, Muawiya took over the caliphate and changed it to a hereditary system within Bani Umayya, and after them came Bani al- Abbas where the caliphs succeeded one after the other either by personal nomination (from the previous caliph) or by means of force and seizure of power. From the beginning of the Islamic era until Kamal Ataturk - who abolished the Islamic caliphate - there has been no correct acclamation[24] except that for the Commander of the Believers 'Ali ibn Abi Talib.

The Prophetic traditions which indicate that 'Ali should be followed

The prophetic traditions which persuaded me to follow Imam 'Ali were those I have read in the Sihahs of the Sunnis and were approved by the Shiites, and they have many more. But as usual I only referred to the prophetic traditions that have been agreed on by both parties, and here are some of them:

1. The Prophetic tradition: "I am the city of Knowledge and 'Ali is its gate."

This tradition[25] alone should be sufficient to indicate the example that has to be followed after the Messenger of Allah (saw) because the educated man ought to be followed.
Allah - the Most High - said:

> "Say: 'Are those who know and those who do not know alike?' (Holy Quran 39:9)

He also said:

> "Is He then who guides to the truth more worthy to be followed, or he who himself does not go aright unless he is guided? What then is the matter with you; how do you judge?" (Holy Quran 10:35)

History has recorded many facts telling us that 'Ali was the most knowledgeable man among all the Companions and they used to consult him on every important matter, and we do not know of any event in which he declined to give his advice.

Abu Bakr said, "May Allah never put me in a predicament that Abu al- Hasan cannot solve." And Umar said, "If it was not for 'Ali, Umar would have perished."[26]

And Ibn Abbas said, "My knowledge and the knowledge of the Companions of Muhammad(saw) is but a drop in seven seas if compared with 'Ali's knowledge."

And this is what Imam 'Ali said about himself, "Ask me before you lose me. By Allah, if you ask me about anything that could happen up to the Day of Judgement, I will tell you about it. Ask me about the Book of Allah, because by Allah there is no (Qur'anic) verse that I do not know whether it was revealed during the night or the day, or whether it was revealed on a plain or on a mountain."[27]

Abu Bakr was once asked about the meaning of the word "Abb" (herbage) in the words of Allah, the Most High:

"And fruits and herbage, A provision for you and for your cattle." (Holy Quran 80:31-32)

Abu Bakr replied, "Which sky would give me shade, and which land would carry me if I say something I do not know about the Book of Allah." And this is Umar saying. "All people are more knowledgeable than I am, even women." He was once asked about the meaning of a Qur'anic verse, and his reaction was to rebuke the man and beat him until he bled, then he said, "Do not ask about matters which may appear bad to you."[28]

Also he was asked about "al-Kalalah" but he did not know what it meant. In his "commentary", al-Tabari stated that Umar once said the following, "My knowledge of al-Kalalah is more valuable to me than owning a palace similar to those in Syria."

In one of his books, Ibn Maja quoted Umar as saying "There are three things, if they were explained by the Messenger of Allah, I would have loved them more dearly than anything in the world: Al-Kalalah, usury and the caliphate." God forbid that the Messenger of Allah stayed silent on these subjects!

1. The Prophetic tradition: "O 'Ali! You hold in relation to me the same position as Haroon held in relation to Moses, except that there shall be no prophet after me."B. The Prophetic tradition: "O 'Ali! You hold in relation to me the same position as Haroon held in relation to Moses, except that there shall be no prophet after me."

This tradition, as should be apparent to every sensible person, shows the special quality of the Commander of the Believers, 'Ali, which made him the right person to be the supporter, the guardian and the deputy (or successor) of the Messenger of Allah as Haroon was the supporter, guardian and deputy of Moses when he went to meet his God. There is also the position of 'Ali vies-a-vies the Prophet which is absolutely equal to the relation between Haroon and Moses, except for the prophethood, which was excluded in the same tradition.

Furthermore, we find in the tradition the fact that Imam 'Ali was the best Companion, who only came second after the Messenger of Allah (saw).

1. The Prophetic tradition: "'Ali is the master of all those of whom I am master. O Allah! Love him who loves him and hate him who hates him, help him who helps him, forsake him who forsakes him, and turn justice with him wherever he turns."

This tradition alone is sufficient to reply to the allegations concerning the seniority of Abu Bakr, Umar and Uthman to 'Ali, who was appointed by the Messenger of Allah as the guardian after him of all the faithful. It is of no consequence for whoever tried to interpret the saying as the friend or the support in order to divert it from its original meaning so that the integrity of the Companions may be kept intact.

The Messenger of Allah stood up in the terrible heat addressing the people, saying, "Do you witness that I have a prior right to and superior authority over all the faithful?" They replied, "Yes, O Messenger of Allah." Thereupon he said, "'Ali is the master of all those whom I am a master etc." This is a clear text indicating that the Messenger of Allah had appointed 'Ali as his successor to lead the nation (of Islam), and the fair and sensible person could not but accept this interpretation and refuse that of the others, thus preserving the integrity of the Messenger of Allah before preserving the integrity of the Companions.

Those who give an alternative interpretation to the saying are in fact ridiculing the wisdom of the Messenger of Allah, who gathered the

multitude of people, in that unbearable heat, to tell them that 'Ali was the friend and supporter of the faithful. And what do those, who misinterpret the text in order to preserve the integrity of their masters, say about the procession of congratulation that the Messenger of Allah organized for 'Ali? It started with the wives of the Messenger, the mothers of the faithful, and then Abu Bakr and Umar came and said to him, "Well done Ibn Abi Talib, Overnight you became the guardian (master) of all the faithful."

In fact all the historical evidence gives clear indications that those who misinterpret the above tradition are liars. Woe to those who wrote what they wrote, and woe to them for what they are writing. Allah, the Most High, said.

"...a party of them most surely conceal the truth while they know it." (Holy Qur'an 2:146)

1. The Prophetic tradition: "'Ali is from me and I am from 'Ali and no one can discharge my duty except myself or 'Ali."D. The Prophetic tradition: "'Ali is from me and I am from 'Ali and no one can discharge my duty except myself or 'Ali."

This honorable tradition[29] is another clear indication that Imam 'Ali was only one whom the Messenger authorized to discharge his duties. The Messenger said it on the day of the great pilgrimage when he sent 'Ali with Surat Bara'a instead of Abu Bakr, who came crying and asked, "O Messenger of Allah! Reveal something for me." The Messenger answered, "My Lord ordered me that nobody can discharge my duty except myself or 'Ali."

There is another supporting tradition that the Messenger of Allah, said on another occasion in honor of 'Ali, "O 'Ali! You will show them the right path when there will be dissension among them after me."[30] If nobody could discharge the Messenger of Allah's duty except 'Ali, and if he was the one who would show them the right path after dissension appeared among them after him; then how could a person who did not know the meaning of "al- Abb" and "Kalalah" be more senior to 'Ali?

This is sadly one of the tragedies that have been inflicted on our nation and prevented it from doing the duties that Allah has chosen for it. We could not blame Allah or the Messenger of Allah or the Commander of the Believers 'Ali ibn Abi Talib for that, but the blame falls squarely on those who rebelled and changed, and Allah, the most High, said:

> *"And when it is said to them, 'Come to what Allah has revealed and to the Messenger.' They say, 'That on which we found our fathers is sufficient for us.' What! Even though their fathers knew nothing and did not follow the right way." (Holy Qur'an 5:104)*

1. The Prophetic tradition of the House on the day of Warning.

The Prophet of Allah (saw) said, indicating 'Ali: "This is my brother, my trustee and my deputy (caliph) after me, so listen to him and obey him."[31]

This is yet another correct tradition cited by many historians at the beginning of the prophetic mission, and considered as one of the Prophet's miracles. However, political intrigues distorted the facts. Then there is no wonder that the oppression which took place then is coming back again in our lifetime. For example, Muhammad Husayn Haykal reproduced the saying in its entirety in his book "The Life of Muhammad", (Page 104, First Edition 1334 Hijri). From the Second Edition onward, the part of the tradition where the Prophet says, "He is my trustee, my deputy (caliph) after me" has been removed.

Also, in al-Tabari's commentary (Tafsir) Volume 19, page 121, when the Prophet says: "My trustee and my deputy (caliph)" was changed to "This is my brother etc. etc", but they failed to recognize that al-Tabari had cited the tradition in its entirety in his Annals Volume 2, Page 319. Look how they change the words and distort the facts...they want to put out the light of Allah with their mouths, but Allah is spreading His light.

During my investigation I wanted to see the truth, so I searched for the first edition of "The Life of Muhammad", and after some hard work, praise be to Allah, found it, although it cost me considerably. The important thing is that I looked at the distortion and became convinced that the evil people are trying the best they can do to remove the facts because there is strong evidence in the hands of their "enemies".

When the fair investigator comes across such a blatant distortion, he will no doubt begin to keep away from them and become convinced that they have no evidence except lies and distorted facts.

They hire writers to whom they give money, titles and false university degrees in order to write for them books and articles through which they insult the Shiites and accuse them of blasphemy, while at the same time they defend the position, even if it is unjust, of some of the Companions who turned on their heels and exchanged right for wrong after the departure of the Messenger of Allah. Allah says:

"Even thus said those before them, the like of what they say; their hearts are all alike. Indeed We have made the verses clear for a people who are sure." (Holy Quran 2:118)

Notes

1. Musnad, Ahmed Hanbal, vol 4 p 281; Siyar al Amin, al Ghazali, p 12; Tadhkirat al Awas, Ibn al Jawzi, p 29; Al Riyadh al Nazarah, al Tabari, vol 2 p 169; al Bidayah wan Nihayah, vol 5 p 212; Tarikh, Ibn Asakir, vol 2 p 50; Tafsir, al Razi, vol 3 p 63; al Hawi lil Fatawi, al Suyuti, vol 1 p 112
2. Tarikh, al Tabari, Ibn al Athir, Suyuti, Baghdadi
3. Tarikh, Qutaybah, vol 1 p 18
4. Sahih, Bukhari, vol 4 p 127
5. Sharh, Muhammad Abduh, vol 1 p 34, Sermon as Shaqshaqiyah
6. Tarikh, Qutaybah, vol 1 p 17
7. al Saqifah wal Khulafah by Abdul Fattah Abdul Maqsood; al Saqifah by Muhammad Rida al Muzaffar
8. Tarikh, Qutaybah, vol 1 p 19; Shahrah, Ibn al Hadid
9. Sahih, Bukhari, vol 3 p 36; Sahih, Muslim, vol 2 p 72
10. With reference to her mounting the Camel during the War of the Camel.
11. With reference to her mounting the mule on the day when she prevented the burial of al Hasan next to his grandfather.
12. Sharh of Nahj al Balagha, Ibn al Hadid, vol 16 p 220-223

13. al Mustadrak, al Hakim, vol 3 p 107; al Manaqib, al Khawarizmi, p 3 and 9; Tarikh, Suyuti, p 168; al Sawaiq al Muhriqah, Ibn Hajjar, p 72; Tarikh, Ibn Asakir, vol 3 p 63; Shawahid at Tanzil, al Haskani al Hanafi, vol 1 p 19.
14. al Riyadh al Nazarah, Tabari, vol 2 p 282; al Sawaiq al Muhriqah, p 118, 72
15. Sahih, Bukhari, vol 2 p 202
16. Fath al Bari (Sharah al Sahih Bukhari), vol 7 p 83; Tarikh, Suyuti, p 199; al Sawaiq al Muhriqah, p 125
17. Muwatta, Malik,. vol 1 p 307; Maghazi, al Waqidi, p 310
18. Sahih, al Tirmidhi, vol 4 p 339; Musnad, Ahmed Hanbal, vol 2 p 319; Mustadrak, al Hakim, vol 3 p 51
19. Sahih, Muslim (Chapter on the virtues of Imam 'Ali (as))
20. Sahih, Bukhari, vol 4 p 184
21. al Imamah was Siyasah, Qutaybah, vol 1 p 14, Treatise, al Jahiz, p 301; A'alam al Nisa, vol 3 p 1215
22. Tarikh, Tabari, vol 4 p 52; al Imamah wa Siyasah, vol 1 p 18; Tarikh, Masudi, vol 1 p 514
23. Tadhkirat al Khawass, Sibt ibn al Jawzi, p 23; Tarikh, Ibn Asakir, vol 1 p 107; al Manaqib, al Khawarizmi, p 7; Al Fusul al Muhimmat, Ibn al Sagh al Maliki, p 21
24. i.e by the consensus of the Muslims
25. Mustadrak, al Hakim, vol 3 p 127; Tarikh, Ibn Kathir, vol 7 p 358
26. al Isti'ab, vol 3 p 39; Manaqib al Khawarizmi, p 48; al Riyadh al Nadirah, vol 2 p 194
27. al Riyadh al-Nadirah, vol 2 p 198; Tarikh, Suyuti, p 124; al Itqan, Suyuti, vol 2 p 319; Fath al Bari, vol 8 p 485; Tadhib al Tadhib, vol 7 p 338
28. Sunan, al Darimi, vol 1 p 54; Tafsir, Ibn Katheer, vol 4 p 232; Tafsir, Suyuti, vol 6p 111
29. Sunan, Ibn Majah, vol 1 p 44; Khasais, al Nasai, p 20; Sahih, al

Tirmidhi, vol 5 p 300; Jami al Usul, Ibn Kathir, vol 9 p 471; al Jami al Saghir, al Suyuti, vol 2 p 56; al Riyadh al Nadirah, Tabari, vol 2p 229

30. Tarikh, Ibn Askir, vol 2 p 488; Kunuz al Haqa'iq, al Mauawi, p 203; Kanz al Ummal, vol 5 p 33
31. Tarikh, al Tabari, vol 2 p319; al Sirah al Halabiyah, vol 1 p 311; Shawahid al Tanzil, vol 1 p 371; Kanz al Ummal, vol 15 p 15; Tarikh, Ibn Asakir, vol 1 p 85; Tafsir, Ala al Din al Shafi'i, vol 3 p 371

The Life of Muhammad by Hasanyn Haykal, First Edition (Section on: And admonish your nearest, your kinsmen)

The Correct Prophetic Traditions Which Indicate the Fact that it is Compulsory to Follow the Ahl al Bayt

The Prophetic tradition of the two weighty things

The messenger of Allah (saw) said: "O People, I leave amongst you two things which if you follow, you will never go astray. They are the Book of Allah and my Ahl al-Bayt (family).

He also said: The messenger of my God is about to come to me and I shall answer. I am leaving with you the two weighty things: The first is the Book of Allah, in which you find guidance and enlightenment, and the people of my household. I remind you, by Allah, of the people of my household...I remind you by Allah of the people of my household."[1]

If we examine with some care this honorable tradition, which has been cited by the Sihahs of the Sunnis and al-Jamaah, we will find that the Shiites alone followed the two weighty things: "The Book of Allah and honorable members of the Prophet's Household." On the other hand, the Sunnis and al- Jamaah followed the saying of Umar "The

Book of Allah is sufficient for us", but I wish they had followed the Book of Allah without interpreting it in their own ways.

If Umar himself did not understand the meaning of al-Kalalah and did not know the Qur'anic verse regarding the Tayammum and other rules, so how about those who came later and followed him without the ability to interpret the Qur'anic texts?

Naturally they will answer me with their own quoted saying, and that is: "I have left with you the Book of Allah and my tradition (Sunnah)."[2]

This tradition, if it were correct, and it is correct in its general meaning, would correspond to the tradition of the two weighty things, because when the Prophet(saw) talked about his Household (Ahl al-Bayt) he meant that they should be consulted for two reasons. Firstly, to teach the tradition (Sunnah), or to transmit to people the correct tradition because they are cleared from telling any lies, and because Allah, praise be to Him, made them infallible in the purification verse.

Secondly to explain and interpret the meanings and aims of the tradition, because the Book of Allah is not enough for guidance; There are many parties who claim to follow the Qur'an but in actual fact they have gone astray, and the Messenger of Allah said, "How many are the readers of the Qur'an whom the Qur'an curses!"

The Book of Allah is silent and could be interpreted in various ways, and it contains what is vague and what is similar, and to understand it we have to refer to those who are well endowed with knowledge as regards the Qur'an, and to Ahl al-Bayt, as regards to the Prophet's traditions.

The Shiites referred everything to the infallible Imams of Ahl al-Bayt (the Prophet's Household), and they did not interpret anything unless it had a supporting text.

We refer in every case to the Companions, whether it concerns Qur'anic commentary or the confirmation of the Sunnah and its explanation, and we know about the Companions and their interpretations and their personal opinions vies-a-vies the clear texts, and there are hundreds of them, so we cannot rely upon them after what they have done.

If we ask our religious leaders, "Which Sunnah do you follow?" They answer categorically, "The Sunnah of the Messenger of Allah!"

But the historical facts are incompatible with that, for they claim that the Messenger of Allah said, "Take my Sunnah and the Sunnah of the Rightly Guided Caliphs after me. Hold firmly to it." But the Sunnah they follow is often the Sunnah of the Rightly Guided Caliphs, and even the Messenger's Sunnah which they claim to follow is in fact transmitted by those people.

However, we read in our Sihahs that the Messenger of Allah prevented them from writing his Sunnah so that it was not confused with the Qur'an. Abu Bakr and Umar did the same thing during their caliphate; we therefore have no proof for the saying, "I left you my Sunnah."[3]

The examples that I have cited in this study, besides many that I have not mentioned, are enough to refute this saying, because there are elements in the Sunnah of Abu Bakr, Umar and Uthman which contradict and negate the Prophet's Sunnah, as is so apparent.

The first incident that took place immediately after the death of the Messenger of Allah, which the Sunnis as well as the historians recorded, was the argument between Fatimah al-Zahra and Abu Bakr regarding the alleged saying, "We, the prophets, do not leave an inheritance, all that we leave behind should go to charity."

Fatimah denied and refuted this saying, with the support of the Book of Allah, and protested against Abu Bakr's allegation and said that her father, the Messenger of Allah, could not contradict the Book of Allah which was revealed to him, for Allah, praise be to Him the Most High, said:

"Allah enjoins you concerning your children. The male shall have the equal of the portion of two females..." (Holy Qur'an 4:11).

This Qur'anic verse is general and is applicable to prophets and non-prophets alike.

She also protested with the following words of the most High:

"And Sulaiman was Dawood's heir" (Holy Qur an 27:16),

and both of them were prophets. Allah, Glory be to Him, also said:

"...Grant me from Thyself an heir, who should inherit from me and inherit from the children of Yaqub, and make him, my Lord, one with whom You are well pleased." (Holy Qur'an 19:5-6)

The second incident that involved Abu Bakr during the early days of his caliphate, which the Sunni historians recorded, was his disagreement with the nearest of all people to him, Umar ibn al-Khattab. The incident revolves around Abu Bakr's decision to fight those who refused to pay Zakat (alms) and kill them, but Umar protested and advised him not to fight them because he had heard the Messenger of Allah saying: I have been ordered to fight the people until they say, "There is no other god but Allah and Muhammad is the Messenger of Allah." And he who says it can keep his wealth to himself and I have no right to his (blood), and he is accountable to Allah.

This is a text cited by Muslim in his Sahih: "The Messenger of Allah (saw) gave the flag to 'Ali on the Day of Khayber, and 'Ali said, 'O Messenger of Allah, what am I fighting them for?' The Messenger of Allah replied, 'Fight them until they testify that there is no other god but Allah and that Muhammad is the Messenger of Allah, and if they do that then they will prevent you from killing them and taking their wealth, except by justice, and they will be accountable to Allah.'[4]

But Abu Bakr was not satisfied with this tradition and said: "By Allah, I will fight those who differentiate between the prayers and Zakat because Zakat is justly charged on wealth." And also said: "By Allah if they refuse me a rope which they used to give to the Messenger of Allah. I will fight them for it." After that Umar ibn al-Khattab was satisfied and said, "As soon as I saw Abu Bakr determined I felt very pleased."

I do not know how Allah could please somebody who is preventing the tradition of the Prophet. This interpretation was used to justify their fight against Muslims although Allah had prohibited making war against them, and Allah said in His Glorious Book:

> *O You who believe! When you go to war in Allah's way, make investigation, and do not say to anyone who offers you peace, "You are not a believer." Do you seek the goods of this world's life? But with Allah there are abundant gains, you too were such before, then Allah conferred a benefit on you; therefore make investigation surely Allah is aware of what you do." (Holy Qur'an 4:94)*

Those who refused to give Abu Bakr their Zakat did not deny its necessity, but they only delayed it to investigate the matter. The Shiites say that these people were surprised by the succession of Abu Bakr, and some of them had been present with the Messenger of Allah at the Farewell Pilgrimage and had heard the text in which he mentioned 'Ali ibn Abi Talib. Therefore they decided to wait for a while until they obtained a clarification as to what had happened, but Abu Bakr wanted to silence them lest they spoke the truth. Because I do not reason with nor protest against what the Shiites say, I will leave this issue to somebody who is interested in it.

However, I should not forget to note here that the Messenger of Allah (saw) had an encounter with Tha'alabah who asked him repeatedly to pray for him to be rich and he promised Allah to give alms. The Messenger of Allah prayed for him and Tha'alabah became so rich that his sheep and camels filled al-Medinah, and he started to neglect his duties and stopped attending the Friday Prayers. When the Messenger of Allah sent some officials to collect the Zakat, he refused to give them anything saying that it was a Jiziah (head tax on free non-Muslims under Muslim rule) or similar to it, but the Messenger of Allah did not fight him nor did he order his killing, and Allah revealed the following verse about him:

> *"And there are those of them who made a covenant with Allah. If He gives us out of His Grace, we will certainly give alms and we will certainly be of the good. But when He gave them out of His Grace, they became niggardly of it and they turned back and they withdrew."(Holy Qur'an 9:75-76)*

After the revelation of the above Quranic verse, Tha'alabah came to the Messenger of Allah crying and asked him to accept his Zakat, but the Messenger of Allah refused to accept it, according to the story.

If Abu Bakr and Umar were following the tradition of the Messenger why did they allow the killing of all these innocent Muslims just because they refused to pay the Zakat?

As for those apologists who were trying to correct Abu Bakr's mistake when he interpreted the Zakat as a just tax on wealth, there is no excuse for them nor for Abu Bakr after considering the story of Tha'alabah who withheld the Zakat and thought of it as "Jiziah". Who knows, perhaps Abu Bakr persuaded his friend Umar to kill those who refused to pay the Zakat because otherwise their call would have spread throughout the Islamic world to revive al-Ghadir's text in which 'Ali was confirmed as successor (to the Messenger of Allah). Thus Umar ibn al-Khattab wanted to fight them, and it was he who threatened to kill and burn those who remained in Fatimah's house in order to extract the acclamation from them for his friend.

The third incident which took place during the early days of Abu Bakr's caliphate in which he found himself in disagreement with Umar, and for which certain Qur'anic and Prophetic texts were interpreted, was that of Khalid ibn al-Walid who killed Malik ibn Nuwayrah and took his wife and married her on the same day. Umar said to Khalid, O enemy of Allah, you killed a Muslim man, then you took his wife ... by Allah, I will stone you."[5] But Abu Bakr defended Khalid, and said, "O Umar, forgive him, he made a mistake, but do not rebuke him."

This is another scandal that history has recorded for a prominent Companion, and when we talk about him, we talk with respect and reverence; we even gave him the title 'The ever drawn sword of Allah." What can I say about a Companion who did all that? Who killed Malik ibn Nuwayrah, the honorable Companion, leader of Bani Tamin and Bani Yarbu, famous for his courage and generosity, and furthermore the historians tell us that Khalid killed Malik and his followers after they put down their arms and stood together to pray.

They were tied by ropes and with them were Leyla bint al-Minhal, wife of Malik, who was considered to be one of the most beautiful Arab ladies of her time, and Khalid was captured by her beauty. Malik said, "O Khalid, send us to Abu Bakr and he will be our judge." And Abdullah ibn Umar together with Abu Qutadah al-Ansari intervened and urged Khalid to send them to Abu Bakr, but he refused and said, "Allah will never forgive me if I do not kill him."

Malik then turned to his wife Leyla and said, "This is the one who will kill me." After that Khalid ordered his execution and took his wife

Leyla and married her that very night.⁶

What can I say about those Companions who trespassed on what Allah deemed to be forbidden; they killed Muslims because of personal whims and permitted themselves to have women that Allah had forbidden us to have. In Islam, a widow cannot be wed by another man before a definite period of time had elapsed, and this period of time has been specified by Allah in His Glorious Book.

But Khalid followed his whims and debased himself, for what would this period of time ('Iddah) mean to him after he had already killed her husband and his followers despite the fact that they were Muslims. Abdullah ibn Umar and Abu Qutadah have testified to this, and the latter became so angry about Khalid's behaviour that he returned to al-Medinah and swore that he would never serve in an army led by Khalid ibn al-Walid.⁷

As we are talking about this famous incident, it is worth looking at what Haykal said in his book "al-Siddiq Abu Bakr" in a chapter entitled "The opinion of Umar and his reasoning on the subject matter": "Umar, who was an ideal example of firm justice, saw that Khalid had dealt unjustly with another Muslim man and took his widow before the end of her ('Iddah), therefore he should not stay in command of the army. So that no such incident would be repeated again and spoil the affairs of the Muslims and give them a bad name amongst the Arabs, he said, 'It is not right to leave him unpunished after his affair with Leyla.'

Let us suppose that it was right that he passed a judgment on Malik but got it wrong, which was something Umar would not permit, what he had done with his widow alone would have meant that he had to be brought to justice.

Furthermore, being the "sword of Allah" and the commander of the victorious army, did not give him the right to do what he had done, otherwise people like Khalid would abuse the law. Worse still, they would be bad examples for all Muslims on how to respect the Book of Allah. Thus Umar kept the pressure on Abu Bakr until he recalled Khalid and rebuked him."[8]

May we ask Mr. Haykel and his like from our scholars, who would compromise in order to preserve the honor of the Companions: Why did Abu Bakr not bring Khalid to justice? And if Umar was an ideal example of firm justice, as Haykel puts it, why did he only remove him from the command of the army, and not bring him to justice so that he would not be a bad example for all Muslims of how to respect the Book of Allah, as he said. And did they respect the Book of Allah and discharge the laws of Allah? Nay! It was politics! It does wonders; it changes the truth and throws the Qur'anic texts over the wall.

Some of our scholars tell us in their books that the Messenger of Allah (saw) once became very angry when Usamah tried to mediate on behalf of an honorable woman accused of stealing, and the Messenger said, "Woe unto you! Do you mediate about one of the laws of Allah? By Allah if it was Fatimah the daughter of Muhammad, I would cut her hand. He destroyed those before you because they would let the thief go if he was an honorable person, but would bring him to justice if he was a weak one."

How could they be silent about the killing of the innocent Muslims, and the marriage of their widows on the same night despite the tragic loss of their husbands? I wish they had remained silent! But they try to justify Khalid's misdeed by inventing various virtues for him, they even called him "The ever drawn sword of Allah" I remember being surprised by a friend of mine, who used to like joking and changing the meaning of the words, when I mentioned the virtues of Khalid ibn al-Walid during my days of ignorance and called him "The ever drawn sword of Allah." He replied, "He is the crippled sword of the devil!"

I was surprised then, but after my research, Allah has opened my eyes and helped me to know the true value of those who seized the caliphate, changed the laws of Allah and violated the boundaries of

Allah.

There is a famous story about Khalid which happened during the lifetime of the Prophet who sent him on a mission to Bani Judhaymah to call them to Islam, but did not order him to fight them. But they did not declare their Islam very well, instead they said, "We are turning to... we are turning (to Islam)." As a result Khalid started to kill them and took prisoners from them, and pushed them towards his friends whom he ordered to kill those prisoners.

But some of his friends refused to do what they were told because they realized that these people had been truly converted to Islam, and they went back and told the Prophet what had happened. He said. "O Allah I am innocent of Khalid's deed." He said it twice,[9] and then sent 'Ali ibn Abi Talib to Bani Judhaymah with money to pay compensation for their dead and for the loss of their wealth, even down to a dog. The Messenger of Allah stood up and faced the Qiblah (the direction of al- Ka'ba) and raised his hands to the sky then said, "O Allah, I am innocent of Khalid's deed three times."[10]

May we ask where the alleged fairness of the Companions, which these people claim to have had, is? If Khalid ibn al-Walid, who is considered to be one of our greatest military leaders, was the sword of Allah, does that mean that Allah drew his sword to kill the innocent Muslims and to violate the integrity of people? There is a clear contradiction here, because Allah forbids the killing of human beings and prohibits the committing of vile deeds, but Khalid seems to have drawn the sword of injustice to kill innocent Muslims and to confiscate their wealth and to take their women.

There is a blatant lie and a clear deception. Praise and thanks he upon You our God, Blessed be You the Most High, Praise be upon You, You did not create the skies and the earth and what is in between them unjustly. These are the doubts of those who blaspheme. Woe to those who committed blasphemy, for Hell is awaiting them. How did Abu

Bakr, who was the caliph of the Muslims, allow himself to listen to all these crimes and be silent about them?

Moreover he asked Umar to stop attacking Khalid and was very angry at Abu Qutadah because he protested strongly about Khalid's action. Was he convinced that Khalid had passed a judgment but got it wrong? What excuse could be given to those corrupt criminals who violated human integrity and claimed to have passed judgment? I do not think that Abu Bakr was trying to pass judgment on Khalid who Umar ibn al-Khattab called "The enemy of Allah".

Umar thought that Khalid should be killed because he had killed an innocent Muslim, or be subjected to a hell of stones because he had committed adultery with Leyla, the widow of Malik. But nothing like that happened to Khalid; rather he defeated Umar because he had the full support of Abu Bakr who knew the whole truth about Khalid more than anybody else.

Historians have recorded that after this terrible misdeed, Abu Bakr sent Khalid on a mission to al-Yamamah, from which he came out victorious and subsequently married a girl from there in the same way as he had Leyla, before the blood of those innocent Muslims and the blood of the followers of Musaylama had dried. Later, Abu Bakr rebuked him about what he had done and used stronger words than those he used during the affair of Leyla.[11]

Undoubtedly, this girl's husband was killed by Khalid who took her for himself, in the same way as he had Leyla, the widow of Malik. It must have been so, otherwise Abu Bakr would not have rebuked him using stronger words than the previous event. The historians mention the text of the letter which Abu Bakr sent to Khalid ibn al-Walid in which he said: "O Ibn Umm Khalid. Upon my life you are doing nothing but marrying women, and in the yard of your house there is the blood of one thousand two hundred Muslims yet to dry!".[12] When Khalid read the letter, he commented, "This must be the work of al-A'sar" meaning Umar ibn al-Khattab.

These are the strong facts that made me shun these types of Companions, and their followers who support them and defend them eagerly and invent various texts and stories to justify the deeds of Abu Bakr, Umar, Uthman, Khalid ibn al-Walid, Muawiyah, Amr ibn al-As and their brethren. O Allah! I am innocent of the deeds and the sayings of those people who opposed Your rules, violated Your prohibitions and trespassed on Your territories. I am innocent of their followers and their supporters, despite their full knowledge of the latter's misdeeds, forgive me for my previous support for them because I was ignorant and Your Messenger said: "He who does not know (the ignorant) cannot be excused for his ignorance."

O Allah! Our leaders have led us astray and veiled the truth from us and presented us with distorted pictures of those renegade Companions and led us to believe that they were the best people after Your Messenger. There is no doubt that our forefathers were victims of the deception and the intrigues of the Umayyads and later the Abbasids.

O Allah! Forgive them and forgive us because You know what is in our inner souls. They loved and respected those Companions out of goodwill assuming that they were supporters of Your Messenger, may Your blessings and peace be upon him and upon those who love him. You know, my Lord their and our love for the purified family, the Imams whom You cleansed and purified and, at their head, the master of all Muslims, the Commander of the Believers, chief of the singularly radiant, Imam of all those who fear Allah our lord 'Ali ibn Abi Talib.

O Allah! Let me be one of their followers who have committed themselves to their cause and followed their path. Let me be on their ship and help me to hold on to their strong link. Let me enter their doors and assist me in dedication to their love, help me to follow their words and their deeds, and let me be grateful to their virtues. O Allah! Let me be with them, for Your Prophet (saw) said, "Man is assembled together (on the day of Judgment) with those whom he loves."

The Prophetic tradition of the Ship

The Messenger of Allah (saw) said: "Behold! My Ahl al-Bayt are like the Ark of Noah, whoever embarked in it was saved, and whoever turned away from it was drowned."[13]

He also said: "My Ahl al-Bayt are like the Gate of Repentance of the children of Israel; whoever entered therein was forgiven."[14]

Ibn Hajjar cited the above tradition in his book "Al-Sawa'iq al-Mahriqa" and gave the following commentary: The idea behind comparing them with the Ark (ship) is to say that whoever loves them and reveres them as a sign of his gratitude for their graces, and whoever is guided by their learned people, will be saved from the darkness of contradictions. On the other hand whoever decides to stay behind, will sink in the sea of ingratitude and will be destroyed in the wilderness of tyranny. The reason for comparing Ahl al- Bayt with the Gate of Repentance is that Allah - the Most High - made the Gate of Repentance (the Gate of Jericho or Jerusalem) a sign of His forgiveness. Similarly, Ahl al-Bayt are the means of Repentance for this nation.

I wish I could ask Ibn Hajjar if he was one of those who went on board the ship and entered the door and was guided by the religious leaders (Ulama), or was he one of those who order what they do not do in practice and contradict their belief. There are many of those unfair people when I ask them or argue with them they say. "We are in a more favorable situation vies-a-vies Ahl al-Bayt and lmam 'Ali than others, we respect and appreciate Ahl al Bayt and nobody can deny their graces and their virtues."

Yes, they say with their tongues what is not in their hearts, or they respect them and appreciate them but follow and imitate their enemies who fought them and contradicted them, or even perhaps on many occasions do not know who Ahl al-Bayt are, and if you ask them who Ahl al-Bayt are, they answer you immediately, "they are the Prophet's wives from whom Allah kept the dirt away and purified them." When I addressed the question to one of those people, he solved the puzzle by giving me the following answer, "All the Sunni people and al-Jama'ah follow Ahl al-Bayt." I was surprised and said, "How could that be?" He answered, "The Messenger of Allah said that we should take half of our religion from this Humayra, meaning Aisha, therefore we took half of the religion from Ahl al-Bayt."

On this basis one could understand their respect and appreciation for Ahl al-Bayt, but when you ask them about the twelve Imams they would only know 'Ali, al-Hasan and al-Husayn from them, and they would not accept the Imamate of al-Hasan nor al-Husayn. Besides, they respect Muawiyah ibn Abi Sufyan who poisoned al-Hasan and killed him (they call Muawiyah "The writer of the Revelations"), and they also respect Amr ibn al-As in the same way as they respect Imam 'Ali.

This is nothing but contradictions and confusion and an attempt to cover the right with the wrong and the light with darkness. For how could the heart of the believer contain the love of Allah and the devil at the same time, and Allah said in His Glorious Book:

> *"You shall not find a people who believe in Allah and the Latter day befriending those who act in opposition to Allah and His Messenger, even though they were their (own) fathers, or their sons or their brothers or their kinsfolk; these are they into whose hearts He has impressed faith and whom He has strengthened with an inspiration from Him: and He will cause them to enter gardens beneath which rivers flow abiding therein; Allah is well-pleased with them and they are well-pleased with Him; these are Allah's party: now*

surely the party of Allah are the successful ones." (Holy Qur'an 58:22).

Allah also said:

"O You who believe! Do not take My enemy and your enemy for friends. Would you offer them love while they deny what has come to you of truth?" (Holy Qur'an 60:1).

The Prophetic tradition: "He who wishes to live like me."

The Messenger of Allah (saw) said: "Whoever wishes to live and die like me, and to abide in the Garden of Eden after death should acknowledge 'Ali as his patron and follow Ahl al-Bayt after me, for they are my Ahl al-Bayt and they have been created out of the same knowledge and understanding as myself. Woe unto those followers of mine who will deny the Ahl al-Bayt their distinctions and who will disregard their relationship and affinity with me. May Allah never let them benefit from my intercession."[15]

As you can see, the above tradition is one of those clear sayings which do not require any interpretation, nor indeed gives any scope for the Muslims to choose, rather, it eliminates any excuse. If he does not follow 'Ali and acknowledge Ahl al-Bayt, the Prophet's Family he will be deprived of the mediation of their grandfather, the Messenger of Allah (saw). It is worth noting here that at the early stage of my research, I felt doubtful about the authenticity of this tradition and I thought it carried a great threat to those who are not in agreement with 'Ali and Ahl al-Bayt, especially when the tradition does not allow any scope for interpretation.

I became rather worried when I read the book "Al-Isabah" in which Ibn Hajjar al-Asqalani gives the following commentary on the tradition:

"I based the tradition on what Yahya ibn Ya'la al-Muharibi had said, and he is feeble." In fact Ibn Hajjar removed some of the doubt that remained in my minds for I thought that Yahya ibn Ya'la al-Muharihi fabricated the tradition and could not be a reliable transmitter.

But Allah - Praise be to Him the Most High - wanted to show me the whole truth. I read a hook entitled Ideological discussions on the writings of Ibrahim al-Jabhan.[16] This book clarified the situation and it became apparent to me that Yahya ibn Ya'la al-Muharibi was a reliable transmitter of Hadith and the two Shaykhs, Muslim and al-Bukhari depended on what he transmitted. I myself followed his case and found that al-Bukhari cited a few traditions transmitted by him regarding the batttle of al-Hudaybiyah, and they were put in Volume 3, Page 31.

Muslim also cited a few traditions in his Sahih Volume 5 in a chapter entitled "The Boundaries" Page 119. Even al-Dhahabi, with all his restrictions, considered him a reliable transmitter, together with the Imams of al-Jurh and al-Ta'deel (criteria applied to Hadiths to find out the reliable and unreliable transmitter), and of course the two Shaykhs (Muslim and al- Bukhari) used him as a reliable reference. So why all this intrigue, falsification and deception about a man who was considered to be a reliable transmitter by the authors of al-Sihah? Is it because he told the truth regarding the necessity to follow Ahl al-Bayt, and was therefore branded by Ibn Hajjar as feeble and weak?

It seems that Ibn Hajjar was unaware of the fact that his writings would become subject to the security of some highly dedicated scholars and that he would be accountable to them for all what he had written. These scholars were able to uncover his prejudice and ignorance because they were guided by the light of the Prophet and Ahl al-Bayt.

I realized later that some of our scholars try hard to cover the truth so that the affairs of the Companions and the caliphs, who were considered to be their leaders and mentors, remain unknown. We see them trying to interpret the correct tradition in their own ways and give them different meanings, or they deny the traditions that contradict their creed, even if they were mentioned in their own books and Sihahs.

At times they remove half or one-third of the prophetic tradition to replace it with something else! Or they may throw doubts about the reliable narrators (of the tradition) because they raise issues that are not to their liking, and on a few occasions they publish them in the first edition (of a book) but remove it from the subsequent editions without giving any indication to justify their action, in spite of the full knowledge of the intelligent readers as to why the saying has been removed!

I have become aware of all these things after conducting meticulous research and investigation, and I have convincing proof to support what I am saying. I wish they would stop giving me all these excuses to justify the actions of those Companions who turned back on their heels, because their views seem to contradict each other and contradict the historical fact. I wish they would follow the just path, even if it was a bitter one, then they would leave their minds and the minds of others in peace.

They claim that some of the early Companions were not reliable transmitters of the Prophet's tradition; therefore they removed what they did not like, especially if these traditions included some of the last instructions of the Messenger of Allah before his death.

Al-Bukhari and Muslim both write about the fact that the Messenger of Allah advised three things on his death-bed:

- Remove all the polytheists from the Arabian Peninsula
- Reward the delegation in the same way as I have done and the narrator then said: "I forgot the third."[17]

It is possible that those Companions who were present at the death-bed and heard the three instructions forgot the third one, when we know that they used to learn by heart a whole epic after hearing it once? No. It is politics that forced them to forget it and not to mention it again. This is indeed another of those comedies organized by the Companions, because there is no doubt what the first instruction of the Messenger of Allah was to appoint 'Ali as his successor, but the narrator did not recite it.

The person who is involved with the investigation about this issue will inevitably sense the undoubtable recommendation for the succession of 'Ali despite all the attempts to cover it or to remove it. Al-Bukhari cited it in his Sahih in a chapter entitled "Al-Wasaya" (The Legacies or the Recommendations); Muslim also cited it in his Sahih and said that the Prophet recommended 'Ali for the succession in the presence of Aisha.[18] Look how Allah shows His light even if the oppressors try to cover it.

I repeat here what I said before; if those Companions were not reliable enough to transmit the recommendations of the Messenger of Allah, then we cannot blame the followers and those who came after them.

If Aisha, the mother of the faithful, could not bear mentioning the name of 'Ali and could not wish him any good, as Ibn Sa'd writes in his Tabaqat,[19] and al-Bukhari in his Sahih in a chapter entitled "The illness of the Prophet and his death", and if she prostrated herself to thank Allah when she heard the news of 'Ali's death, then how can we expect her to mention the recommendation in favor of 'Ali, when she was known, publicly and privately, for her animosity and hatred towards 'Ali and his sons and towards all the Family of the Prophet. Behold! There is no might or power except in Allah the Most High, the Great.

Notes

1. Sahih, Muslim, Chapter on the Virtues of Imam 'Ali (as), vol 5 p 122, Sahih, al Tirmdhi, vol 5 p 328, Mustadrak, al Hakim, vol 3 p 148 Musnad, Ahmed Hanbal, vol 3 p 17
2. The saying is cited in al Nisa'i, al Tirmdhi, Ibn Majah and Abu Dawood
3. The term 'my Sunnah' does NOT appear in all the six sihahs. It appears in al Muwatta by Malik ibn Anas, some of the subsequent writers, such as al Tabari and Ibn Hisham referred to the saying as transmitted by Malik.
4. Muslim, Sahih, vol 8 p 151
5. Tarikh, Tabari, vol 3 p 280, Tarikh, al Yaqubi, vol 2 p 110, Tarikh, al Fida, vol 1 p 158, al Isabah fi Marifat as Sahabah, vol 3 p 336
6. Tarikh, al Fida, vol 1 p 158, Tarikh, al Yaqubi, vol 2 p 110, Tarikh, Ibn al Shinanah, vol 11 p 114 (On the margin of al Kamil, vol 2 p 114)
7. Tarikh, Tabari, vol 3 p 280, Tarikh, al Fida, vol 3 p 336, Tarikh, al Yaqubi, vol 2 p 110
8. Al Siddiq al Akbar, Haykal, p 151
9. Sahih, Bukhari, vol 4 p 171
10. Sirah, Ibn Hisham, vol 4 p 53, Tabaqat, Ibn Sa'd, Usud al Ghabah, vol 3 p 102
11. Al Siddiq al Akbar, Haykal. p 151
12. Tarikh, Tabari, vol 3 p 254, Tarikh al Khamis, vol 3 p 343
13. Mustadrak, al Hakim, vol 3 p 151

Yanabi Muwaddah, Qundoozi Hanafi, p 30, 370 , al Sawaiq al Muhriqah, Ibn Hajjar, p 184, 234, Majmaa al-Zawaed, al-Haithami, v9, p168

1. 1. Majmaa al-Zawaed, al-Haithami, v9, p168, 2. al-Sawaeq al-

Muhriqa, ibn Hajjar al-Haithami, p193 also in:, 3. Noor al-Absar, al-Shiblinji, 4. al-Ifrad, al-Darqutni

2. Mustadrak, al Hakim, vol 3 p 128, Kanz al Ummal, vol 6 p 155, al Manaqib, Khawarizmi, p 34, Yanabi al Muwaddah, p 149, Tarikh, Ibn Asakir, vol 2 p 95, Hilyat al Awlia, vol 1 p 86 Al Jami al Kabir, al Tabrani and al Isabah, Ibn Hajjar
3. Mubaqasha Aqa diyya fi Maqdat Ibrahim al Jabhan, p 29
4. Sahih, Bukhari, vol 7 p 121, Sahih, Muslim, vol 5 p 75
5. Sahih, Bukhari, vol 3 p 68, Sahih, Muslim, vol 2 p 14
6. Tabaqat, Ibn Sa'd, vol 2 p 29

Our Misfortune Regarding Ijtihad Against the Texts

I gathered through my research that the misfortune which has befallen the Islamic nation has been due to the Companions' interpretation of Islam against the clear texts. Thus they violated the ordinances of Allah and obliterated the Tradition and the religious scholars and leaders who followed their example often contradicted the Prophetic Texts if they did not comply with what one of the Companions had done before them.

At times they even contradicted the Qur'anic Texts, and I am not exaggerating here, and I mentioned earlier in this book the case concerning the "al-Tayammum" verse. Despite the fact that there is a clear text in the Book of Allah as well as in the Messenger's tradition about Tayammum, they still took the liberty of interpreting it, and said that one should abandon the prayers if there was no water. Abdullah ibn Umar justified this interpretation in the way we have encountered elsewhere in this hook.

One of the first Companions to open the door of Ijtihad (interpretation) was the second Caliph who used his discretion vies-a-vies the Qur'anic Texts after the death of the Messenger of Allah (saw) to stop the shares of those whose hearts inclined (to truth), although Allah had made its payment compulsory out of the Zakat, and said, "We do not need you."

As for his interpretation of the Prophetic texts, they are numerous, and on many occasions he contradicted the Prophet himself when he was alive. We have indicated in another chapter his opposition during the peace treaty of al-Hudaybiah, and how strongly he opposed the writing of the Messenger's last recommendation and said that the Book of Allah was sufficient.

There is another incident involving the Messenger of Allah and Umar which shows clearly the latter's mentality and how he allowed himself to argue and oppose the Messenger. The incident was about spreading the good news of Heavens. The Messenger of Allah sent Abu Hurayrah with the instruction that whenever he met a man who is absolutely convinced that "There is no other god but Allah" he was to give him the good news that he would end up in Heaven. Abu Hurayrah duly went out to spread the good news until he met Umar who prevented him from continuing his mission and beat him as he lay on the ground.

Abu Hurayrah went back crying to the Messenger of Allah and told him about his encounter with Umar, so the Messenger asked Umar, "What made you do that?" Umar replied by asking the question, "Did you send him to spread the good news of Heaven to whoever convincingly believes that there is no other god but Allah!" The Messenger of Allah said, "Yes." Umar then said, "Do not do that, because I fear that all the people will rely on there is no other god but Allah."

We also have his son Abdullah ibn Umar who feared that people would rely on al-Tayammum, so he ordered them to abandon the prayers. I wish they had left the texts as they are and that they had not changed them with their futile interpretations which could only lead to the eradication of the Islamic laws, the violation of Allah's sanctity and the division of this nation into various creeds and warring factions.

Looking at the various stances that Umar took regarding the Messenger of Allah and his Tradition we could deduce that he never believed in the infallibility of the Messenger; and he thought of him as any other man subject to right or wrong. Thus comes the opinion adopted by the Sunni scholars and al-Jamaah that the Messenger of Allah was infallible as regards the transmitting the Holy Qur'an, but that apart from that he was like any other human being, sometimes wrong and sometimes right.

Some ignorant people claim that the Messenger of Allah (saw) accepted the temptations of the devil in his home. Once he was lying on his back surrounded by women playing their tambourines and the devil sat joyfully next to him until Umar came, then the devil ran away and the women hid their tambourines under their seats. The Prophet said to Umar, "As soon as the devil saw you, he left by a different way from the way you came in."

It is not therefore surprising that Umar has his own views on the religion and allowed himself to argue with the Messenger of Allah about political issues as well as religious ones, as we explained before regarding the good news about Heaven. From the idea of Ijtihad and using one's own opinion vies-a-vies the texts, a group of Companions, led by Umar ibn al-Khattab, started gathering force, and we saw on "The Day of Misfortune" how they supported Umar's point of view rather than the clear text.

We can then also deduce that it was the same group that did not accept the "al-Ghadir" text in which the Prophet (saw) made it clear that 'Ali would be his caliph (successor) over all the Muslims and they waited for the right opportunity to reject it when the Prophet died. The meeting at "al-Saqeefah" and the subsequent election of Abu Bakr was a result of that Ijtihad, and when they completed their control over the affairs, people started to forget about the Prophetic texts regarding the succession to the caliphate and started to interpret everything.

They challenged the Book of Allah, they violated the boundaries and changed the rules. There was the tragedy of Fatimah al-Zahra after the tragedy of her husband and his removal from the caliphate. There was also the tragedy in the payment of Zakat and the interpretation of that case despite the clear texts.

Then came the succession of Umar to the caliphate which was an inevitable result of Ijtihad, because Abu Bakr implemented his own interpretation of the situation and dropped the Shura (the consultative council) which always used to help him with the running of the caliphate's affairs. After that Umar came and made things even worse, he permitted things which were forbidden by Allah and His Messenger[1] and forbade what Allah and His Messenger had permitted.[2]

When Uthman came to power after Umar, he went a long way in al- Ijtihad, and did more than any on his predecessors had done, until his opinions started to affect political and religious life generally, thus leading to the revolution, and he paid with his life as a price for his Ijtihad.

When Imam 'Ali took charge of the Muslims' affairs he encountered great difficulties in trying to persuade people to go back to the honorable Prophetic Tradition and the Holy Qur'an, and tried his best to rid Islam from all the new innovations, but some people shouted loudly, "Behold! Umar's Tradition!"

I am convinced that those who fought and contradicted Imam 'Ali (as) did so because he forced them to go back to the correct texts. Thus he eradicated all the new innovations and interpretations that had been attached to the religion for the previous quarter of a century to which people had become accustomed, especially those who had their own whims and greed and who used the wealth of Allah and the people for their own ends, and deprived the ordinary folks of the basic rights of Islam.

We always find that self-opinionated individuals tend to favor Ijtihad because it allows them to reach their end by any means to hand, and the texts appear as barriers in their way and prevent them from achieving their goals.

It is worth noting here that Ijtihad may have its followers among the ordinary people, at any time and at any place simply because it is easy to implement and has no firm commitments.

Because the text demands commitments and lacks freedom, politicians tend to call it theocracy, which means the rule of Allah; but Ijtihad, with its freedom and its lack of commitment, is called democracy, meaning the rule of people. The men who met in al-Saqeefah after the death of the Prophet (saw) decided to abolish the theocratic government which was established by the Messenger of Allah on the basis of the Qur'anic texts, and changed it to a democratic government chosen by the people. However, these Companions were not aware of the word "democracy", for it is not an Arabic word, but they knew the "Shura" system.[3]

Those who do not at present accept the text regarding the succession to the caliphate are the proud supporters of "democracy", claiming that Islam was the first to adopt such a system, and they are the supporters of Ijtihad and reforms, and today they are considered to be the nearest possible thing to the western system, and that is why the western governments glorify them and call them the progressive and tolerant Muslims.

The Shiites, who support theocracy or the government of Allah, refuse Ijtihad vis-a-vis the text, and differentiate between the rule of Allah and the Shura. They do not see any connection between the Shura and the Texts, but their main concern is about Ijtihad and the Shura in issues that do not have texts.

We see that Allah, praise be to Him, chose His Messenger Muhammad but He still said to him:

"And consult them about the matter." (Holy Qur'an 3:159)

As for the choice of the leaders of the people, Allah said:

"And your Lord creates and chooses whom He pleases, to choose is not theirs." (Holy Qur'an 28:68)

When the Shiites advocate for the succession of 'Ali to the caliphate after the Messenger of Allah, they are actually committing themselves to the text, and when they discredit some of the Companions, they do it with regard to a few who replaced the text with Ijtihad and thus lost the rule of Allah and His Messenger and opened a wound in Islam that has not yet healed.

As a result we find the western governments and their thinkers despise the Shiites and call them religious fanatics and reactionaries because they want to go back to the Qur'an which rules that the thief should have his hands cut off, and the adulterer should be stoned, and urge people to go and fight in the name of Allah, but all that is haughtiness and barbarism, as far as they are concerned.

Throughout this study I started to comprehend the reason why some of the religious leaders of the Sunni tradition and al-Jamaah closed the gate of Ijtihad as far back as the second Hijri century. Perhaps they predicted the repercussions of Ijtihad on the Islamic nation from misfortunes to bloody civil wars, and how it would change a nation, about which Allah said, "You are the best nation that has come out to the people" to a nation of warring factions where anarchy rules and eventually turns from Islam to the Jahiliya (pre-Islamic period).

Ijtihad continued with the Shiites, as long as the texts remained intact and nobody could change them, and what helped them in that was the Twelve Imams who inherited their grandfather's knowledge, and used to say that there was no problem that did not have Allah as its judge and that the Messenger of Allah (saw) had made it clear.

We also understand that when the Sunni traditionists and al-Jamaah followed the Companions who undertook Ijtihad and prevented the writing of the prophetic tradition found themselves compelled, due to the absence of the texts, to use personal interpretation, Qiyas (analogy), Istishab (association), as well as closing the field of Dhara'i (pretext) and many other measures.

We also understand that the Shiites gathered around Imam 'Ali, who was the gate to the city of knowledge, and he used to say to them, "Ask me about anything, for the Messenger of Allah taught me about one thousand (doors) of knowledge, each one of which opens one thousand more doors."[4] But the non-Shiites gathered around Muawiya ibn Abi Sufyan who knew little about the Prophetic Tradition.

After the death of Imam 'Ali, the leader of the unjust faction became the commander of the believers, and he abused Islam through the implementation of his own personal opinions, which caused more damage to Islam than anybody else before him. But the Sunni traditionists and al- Jamaah say that he was "The writer of the Revelations", and that he was one of the outstanding scholars in the interpretation of Islam. How could they judge him like that when he was the one who poisoned al-Hasan ibn 'Ali, leader of Heaven's youth? Perhaps they say, "This was an aspect of his Ijtihad (interpretation), but he got it wrong!"

How could they judge his Ijtihad, when he was the one who took the nation's acclamation for himself by force, then gave it to his son Yazid after him, and changed the Shura system to a hereditary one?

How could they judge his Ijtihad and give him a reward, when he was the one who forced people to curse 'Ali and Ahl al-Bayt, the offspring of the Prophet, in every mosque, so that it became a followed tradition for sixty years?

And how could they call him "The writer of the Revelations" since the revelation came upon the Messenger of Allah (saw) for twenty-three years, and Muawiyah was a polytheist for the first eleven years of them, and later, when he was converted to Islam, did not live in Medina (for we could not find any historical reference to support that), whereas the Messenger of Allah (saw) did not live in Mecca after al-Fath (the conquer of Mecca by the Muslims)? So how could Muawiya manage to write the Revelation?

Behold! There is no power except in Allah, the Most High, the Great. And the question comes back, yet again: which group was right and which one was wrong? Either 'Ali and his followers were wrong or Muawiyah and his followers were wrong.

The Messenger of Allah (saw) explained everything. but some of those who claim to follow the tradition got it wrong, for it has become apparent to me through the research that the people who defend Muawiyah could only be the followers of Muawiyah and the Umayyads and not, as they claim, the followers of the Prophetic Tradition (Sunnah). If we observe their positions, we find that they hate the followers of 'Ali, and celebrate the Day of Ashura as being a festival and defend the Companions who hurt the Messenger of Allah during his lifetime and after his death, and always correct their mistakes and find justifications for their actions.

How could you love 'Ali and Ahl al-Bayt and at the same time you bless their enemies and their killers? How could you love Allah and His Messenger and at the same time defend those who changed the rules of Allah and His Messenger and interpret these rules in their own way?

How could you respect those who did not respect the Messenger of Allah and accused him of Hajjr and criticized his leadership?

How could you follow religious leaders that have been appointed by the Umayyads and the Abbasids for political reasons, and leave other religious leaders although the Messenger of Allah pointed out their number[5] and their names?[6]

How could you follow somebody who did not know the Prophet very well and leave the gate to the city of knowledge, whose relation to the Messenger was the same as the position of Harun to Musa?

Who was the first to use the term Ahl al-Sunnah (Sunni Traditions) and al-Jamaah? I have searched through the history books and found that they agreed to call the year in which Muawiyah seized power "the year of al- Jamaah".

It was called thus because the nation became divided into two factions after the death of Uthman: The Shi'a of 'Ali and the followers of Muawiyah. When Imam 'Ali was martyred and Muawiyah seized power after his pact with Imam Hasan which enabled him to become commander of the believers the years was then called "al-Jamaah". Therefore the name Ahl al-Sunnah (Sunnah Traditionists), and al-Jamaah indicates the Sunnah (tradition) of Muawiyah, and the agreement on his leadership, and does not mean the followers of the Sunnah (tradition) of the Messenger of Allah.

The Imams and other members of Ahl al-Bayt, who are the descendants of the Messenger of Allah, know more than anybody else about the Sunnah (tradition) of their grandfather and what it entails, for as the proverb goes. The people of Mecca know its paths better than anyone else. But we opposed the Twelve Imams whom the Messenger of Allah mentioned in his sayings and followed their enemies.

Despite our acknowledgement of the tradition in which the Messenger of Allah mentioned twelve caliphs, all of them from Quraysh, we always stop at the four caliphs. Perhaps it was Muawiyah who called us Ahl al-Sunnah and al-Jamaah, meaning the agreement on his Sunnah (tradition) in which he made it compulsory to curse 'Ali and Ahl al-Bayt.

This continued for sixty years until Umar ibn Abdul Aziz - may Allah be pleased with him - stopped it. Some historians inform us that the

Umayyads themselves plotted to kill Umar ibn Abdul Aziz, and he was one of them, because he killed the Sunnah, which was the cursing of 'Ali ibn Abi Talib.

O my people! Let us go - guided by Allah, the Most High - and search for the truth and rid ourselves from that blind prejudice, because we are the victims of the Abbasids and the victims of the dark history and the intellectual barrenness which we have been subjected to for a long time.

Undoubtedly we are the victims of the cunning and the shrewdness of people like Muawiyah, Amr ibn al-As, al-Mughirah ibn Sh'bah and others. Research into our Islamic history in order to reach the absolute truth and Allah will reward you twice. Let us hope that we can unite this nation which was stricken by the death of its Prophet and then became divided into seventy-three factions.

Let us unite this nation under the banner of "There is no other god but Allah, and Muhammad is the Messenger of Allah" and to follow Ahl al-Bayt, whom the Messenger of Allah commanded us to follows and said, "Do not be in front of them, for you will perish, and do not keep away from them, for you will perish, and do not teach them, for they know more than you do?"[7]

If we do that, Allah will lift His anger from us, and He will change our fear to peace and tranquility. and will enable us to rule on this earth, and will make His friend Imam al-Mahdi - may peace be upon him, appear to us, since the Messenger of Allah promised us with his re-appearance to fill the earth with peace and justice after it had been filled with injustice and oppression…thus Allah will complete, through him, the enlightenment of the whole world.

Notes

1. As in the case of the divorce by three times Muslim, Sahih, Chapter on the divorce by three times Sunan, Abi Dawood, vol 1 p 344
2. As in the case of his prohibition of Muta al Hajj and Muta al Nisa Sahih, Muslim, Chapter on Hajj Sahih, Bukhari, Section on al Hajj Chapter on al-Tamattu
3. In fact such thing doesn't happen even in this type of election, because those who are elected are not entitled to represent any nation, in any form.
4. Tarikh Dimashq, Ibn Asakir, vol 2 p 484, Maqt al Husayn, al Khawarizmi, vol 1 p 38, al Ghadir, al Amini, vol 3 p 120
5. Sahih, Bukhari, vol 4 p 164, Sahih, Muslim, p 119
6. Yanibul Muwaddah, al Qunduzi al Hanafi
7. al Durr al Manthur, Suyuti, vol 2 p 60, Usd al Ghabah, vol 3 p 137, al Sawaiq al Muhriqah, Ibn Hajjar, p 148, 226, Kanz al Ummal, vol 1 p 168, Majma az Zawaid, vol 9 p 163

An Invitation to Friends to Join the Research

The change was the beginning of a spiritual happiness for me, and I sensed an inner silence with great joy for the right creed that I had discovered, and had no doubt that it was the true Islam. I felt ecstatic and proud of myself for what Allah had granted me from His guidance and direction.

I could not bear the silence and the secrecy about what was going on inside me, and I said to myself, "I have got to tell the truth to people." "Talk about the graces of your Lord", and it is one of the greatest graces, or indeed, it is the greatest grace in this world and the life hereafter, and "he who keeps silent about the truth is a dumb devil" and "after the truth there is nothing to go astray."

What made me convinced that I should spread this truth was the innocence of those Sunni traditionists and al-Jamaah who love the Messenger of Allah and Ahl al-Bayt, and all what needs to be done is to remove that mist which was made by history and then they would follow the right path, and that is what happened to me personally.

Allah, the Most High, said,

> "... You too were such before, then Allah conferred on you a benefit." (Holy Qur'an 4:94)

Within a month we finished the book, and the three friends were enlightened and I supported them and helped them along the way and gave them all that I had accumulated from experience and knowledge during the years of investigation. I started to taste the sweetness of guidance and became very hopeful about the future.

Frequently, I invited friends from Gafsa who I used to know through the mosque's school or the Sufi orders in addition to some of my faithful students. A year passed, and praise be to Allah, we became a large number. We were all friends of Ahl al-Bayt. We are the friends of their friends, and the enemy of their enemies, we celebrate their festivals and mourn during Ashura.

Two of my early letters which carried the news of my enlightenment were sent to al-Sayyid al-Khu'i and al-Sayyid Muhammad Baqir al-Sadr, during the festivity of al-Ghadir, which we celebrated for the first time in Gafsa. Everybody got to know about my conversion to Shiism and that I was calling people to follow Ahl al-Bayt, and all sorts of accusations and rumors started to go around the country.

I was accused of being an Israeli spy working to make people doubt their religion, that I cursed the Companions and was planning to cause disturbances among the people ... etc. In the capital Tunis I approached two friends, Rashid al-Ghannushi and Abdul Fattah Moro, who expressed strong opposition to my ideas. and in a conversation that took place in Abdul Fattah's house I said that as Muslims, we ought to re-read our hooks and look again at our history, and I gave Sahih al-Bukhari as an example, for it contains materials that any sensible person would find difficult to accept.

They became very angry with me and said, "Who are you to criticize al- Bukhari?" I did my best to persuade them to be involved in the research, but they refused, saying, "If you yourself have become Shi'i, that is your business, but do not try to convert us to Shi'ism. We have a more important task than that: namely to resist the government which does not work according to Islam."

I answered by saying, "What is the use? If you come to power, you will do more than they are doing now, because you do not know the true Islam." Thus our meeting ended with a state of aversion between us.

Some people from The Muslims Brotherhood ran a campaign against us, because they were not aware at that time of the Islamic Trend Movement, and started to spread rumors among their ranks that I was a government agent and that I was encouraging Muslims to doubt their religion in order to keep them away from the main issue: namely resisting the government.

Gradually people started to make us feel isolated, especially the young members of the Muslims Brotherhood and the Shaykhs who follow Sufi ways, and we experienced difficult times, living like strangers in our own homes and among our own brothers.

But Allah - praise be to Him - changed our situation for the better, and many young people from various cities came to see us to investigate the truth, and I tried my utmost to persuade them, and as a result many young men were able to see the light; they were from Tunis, Kayrawan, Susa and Sidi Bu Zayd. During my summer visit to Iraq I travelled through Europe and met friends in France and Holland and discussed the subject with them, and praise be to Allah, they too saw the light.

I was absolutely delighted when I met al-Sayyid Muhammad al-Sadr at his house in Holy Najaf where he was surrounded by a group of learned people. He introduced me to them as being the seeds of Shi'ism (following Ahl al-Bayt) in Tunis. He also told them that he had cried when he first received my letter which carried the news that we had celebrated the festival of al-Ghadir, and how I complained about the difficulties we were facing including malicious rumors and isolation.

Al-Sayyid said: It is inevitable that we pass through difficult times because the path of Ahl al-Bayt is a difficult one. A man once came to see the Prophet (s.a.w.) and said to him, "O Messenger of Allah, I love you." He replied, "Then expect many tribulations." The man said, "I love your cousin 'Ali." He replied, "Then expect many enemies." The man said, "I love al- Hasan and al-Husayn." He replied, "Then get ready for poverty and much affliction."

What have we paid for the cause of justice for which Abu Abdullah al- Husayn (as) paid his life and the lives of his family's members and companions; and for which the Shi'is along the path of history have paid and are still paying up to the present day as a price for their allegiance to Ahl al-Bayt? My Brother, it is inevitable that we go through difficulties and give sacrifices for the cause of justice, and if Allah helped you in guiding one man to the right path, it is worth the whole world and what is within it.

Al-Sayyid al-Sadr also advised me against isolating ourselves and ordered me to get even closer to my Sunni brothers whenever they wanted to keep away from me, and to pray behind them so that there would be no rupture in relations, and to consider them innocent victims of distorted history and bad propaganda, because people are the enemy of what they do not know.

Al-Sayyid al-Khu'i also advised me on the same lines, and al-Sayyid Muhammad 'Ali al-Tabatabai al-Hakim had always sent us letters full of advice that had a great influence on enlightened brothers.

My visits to the Holy City of Najaf and its learned people became more frequent, and I committed myself to spend each summer holiday near Imam 'Ali and attend the lessons of al-Sayyid Muhammad Baqir al-Sadr, from which I reaped great benefits.

I also promised myself to visit the graves of all the twelve Imams and Allah helped me to realize my wish for I was even able to visit the

grave of al-Imam al-Rida which is situated in Mashhad, on the borders between the
U.S.S.R. and Iran. There I met some of the most outstanding scholars, from whom I benefited a great deal.

Al-Sayyid al-Khu'i, whom we follow in our religious affairs, gave me permission to use Khums and Zakat to help our enlightened group, and to give them what they needed regarding books and grants and many other things. I also was able to establish a small library which contained some important references connected with the research which belonged to both parties (Sunnis and Shiis). I called it "Ahl al-Bayt Library" and benefited many people, praise be to Allah.

Fifteen years ago Allah doubled my joy when the clerk to the city council of Gafsa agreed to naming the street where I live "Imam 'Ali ibn Abi Talib (as) Street". I would like to take this opportunity to thank him for that honorable gesture, for he is one of the hard-working Muslims and has a great respect and love for Imam 'Ali, and I presented him with "al- Murajaat" by Sharaf al-Din. He and our group have mutual respect and love for each other, so may Allah reward him well and grant him whatever he wishes.

There were some wicked people who tried to remove the street's sign, but all their attempts were in vain and Allah willed it to stay where it was, and we received letters from all over the world carrying the name of Imam 'Ali ibn Abi Talib's street, whose honourable name blessed our good city.

In accordance with the advice of Ahl al-Bayt (as) and the advice of the learned scholars of the holy city of Najaf we are determined to keep in touch with our brothers from the other madhahibs and have maintained our relation with al-Jamaah by praying together. Thus people started asking us about our prayers, ablution and our beliefs.

The Guidance of Truth

In a small village in the south of Tunisia, during a wedding ceremony, an old lady sat in the middle of a group of ladies listening to them talking about a married couple. The lady expressed her astonishment about what she heard, and when she was asked why, she said that she had breast-fed both when they were babies. The ladies spread the news quickly among their husbands who investigated the matter. The woman's father testified that the old lady had actually breast-fed his daughter, and the man's father also testified that his son was breast-fed by the same old lady.

Inevitably the two tribes were agitated by the news and started fighting each other, and each tribe accused the other of being the cause of this tragedy which would bring the wrath of Allah on them. What made it worse was the fact that that marriage had taken place ten years earlier and had produced three children. As soon as the woman heard the news she fled to her father's house and refused to eat or drink anything, and she attempted suicide for she could not bear the shock of being married to her brother and giving birth to three children without knowing the real situation.

As a result of the clashes between the two tribes, many people were injured until one particular Shaykh intervened and stopped the fighting and advised them to consult the learned scholars and ask them for their opinion in the matter and hopefully they could reach a solution.

The people concerned embarked on their journey around the big town asking the learned people for a solution to their problems. However every time they explained the case to a learned scholar and asked him for advice, he told them that the marriage was void and the couple should be separated for as long as they lived, in addition to freeing a slave or fasting for two months and various other legal opinions.

Eventually they arrived at Gafsa and asked the learned people there but the answer was the same, because all the Malikis prohibit the marriage between a couple if they were fed even one drop of milk from the same woman. They do so by following Imam Malik who treated milk and alcohol on the same level and said, "When a great quantity of whatever makes you drunk is prohibited, then a small amount of it must also be prohibited."

Thus, marriage between couples who were breast-fed with one drop of milk from the same woman must be prohibited. One of the men who was present at the hearing told them privately to come and see me, and he said to them, "Ask al-Tijani on these matters for he knows all the Madhhabs, and on many occasions I had seen him arguing with these learned scholars and beating them with his logical reasoning."

That is what the husband of that woman told me when I took him to my library where he told me the whole case in detail, and said to me, "Sir, my wife wants to commit suicide and our boys are neglected and we do not know how we can solve this problem, and people led us to you hoping that you might have an answer to our problem, especially since I see all these books in your possession, which I have never seen before in my life."

I brought him some coffee and thought about the case for a little while then I asked him about the number of times that he was breast-fed from that old woman. He said, "I do not know, but my wife was breast-fed by her twice or three times and her father testified that he took his daughter two or three times to that old woman."

I said, "if that is right, then there is no problem and your marriage is legal and valid." The poor man fell on me kissing my hands and head, saying, "May Allah bring you good news for you opened the gates of peace to me." Before even finishing his coffee or asking me for any reference, he asked permission to leave my house and hurriedly went out to tell his wife and children and the rest of his family about the good news.

But the day after he came back with seven men and introduced them to me saying, "This is my father, this is my father-in-law, the third is the mayor of the village, the fourth is the Imam of the Friday prayers, the fifth is the religious adviser, the sixth is the chief of the tribe and the seventh is the headmaster of the school, and all of them came to investigate the case of the breast-feeding and how you considered the marriage to be valid."

I took the whole party to the library, and greeted them and offered them coffee for I expected a lengthy debate with them.

They said, "We came to discuss with you how you legalized a marriage in which the couple were breast-fed from the same woman. Such a marriage has been forbidden by Allah in the Qur'an and by His Messenger who said that it (marriage) is forbidden between a couple who have been breast-fed (by the same woman) in the same way as it is forbidden between a couple who are related (brother and sister). Imam Malik has forbidden it too."

I said, "Gentlemen, you are eight and I am one, and if I speak to all of you, I will not be able to convince you and the discussion might well lose its aim. I suggest you choose one man from among you to discuss the matter with me, and you will act as an arbitrator between us."

They liked the idea and chose the religious advisor as their representative because they thought he was more knowledgeable and more able than anybody else. The man started his deliberation by asking me how I allowed something that had been forbidden by Allah, His Messenger and by all the Imams.

I said, "God forbid! I never did such thing. But Allah forbade the marriage (in case of common breast-feeding) by stating it briefly in a Qur'anic verse and did not specify the details; rather, He left it to His Messenger to explain how and how much."

He said, "Imam Malik forbids the marriage when one drop of milk has been taken through breast-feeding."

I said, "I know that. But Imam Malik is not an absolute authority over all Muslims, and what do you say about the opinions of other Imams?"

He said, "May Allah he pleased with them, they all followed the steps of the Messenger of Allah."

I said, "What is then your reasoning before Allah about following Imam Malik who contradicted a text by the Messenger of Allah (saw)?"

He looked bemused and said, "Praise be to Allah! I did not know that Imam Malik could contradict the Prophetic texts."

The rest of the men looked even more puzzled and were amazed at my daring criticism of Imam Malik, which they had never heard before. I continued by asking, "Was Imam Malik one of the Companions?"

He replied, "No." I asked, "Was he one of the Followers?" He replied, "No, but he followed the earlier Followers." I asked, "Who is nearer, him or Imam 'Ali ibn Abi Talib?" He replied, "Imam 'Ali ibn Abi Talib was one of the rightly guided caliphs." One of the men added, "Our master 'Ali (a.s.) is the gate to the city of knowledge." I said, "Why did you leave the gate to the city of knowledge and follow a man who was neither a Companion nor a Follower, and he was born after the civil war and after the city of the Messenger of Allah had been sacked by Yazid's forces who killed the best of the Companions and violated all aspects of human morality and changed the Messenger's tradition to some heretical doctrines of their own make. How could then for any man have confidence in these Imams who pleased the authorities because they preached in accordance to their policies?"

Another man started talking saying, "We heard that you are a Shi'i, and that you worship Imam 'Ali." His friend, who sat next to him, kicked him, and said, "Be quiet, are you not ashamed of yourself saying that to such a learned man? I have known many learned scholars in my life, but I have never known any of them to possess a library like this one. Furthermore, this man's argument is based on knowledge and he sounds sure about what he is saying." I answered, "Yes, that is right, I am a Shi'i, but the Shi'is do not worship 'Ali, but instead of following Imam Malik, they follow Imam 'Ali because he is the gate to the city of knowledge, as you yourselves said."

The religious adviser asked, "Did Imam 'Ali permit the marriage between couples who have been breast-fed by the same woman?"

I answered, "No, he forbids it if the babies were breast-fed fifteen full and consecutive times by the same woman, or what could produce flesh and bone."

The woman's father was very pleased to hear what I had said, and his face lit then he said, "Praise be to Allah! My daughter was breast-fed on two or three occasions by that old woman. The saying of Imam 'Ali is a solution to our predicament and a mercy on us from Allah after we had lost hope."

The religious adviser said, "Give us the authentic reference to the saying (of Imam 'Ali) so that we may feel satisfied. I gave them "MinHajj al- Salihin" by al-Sayyid al-Khu'i, and he read aloud the chapter concerning breast-feeding and what it entails.

The men were very pleased, especially the husband, who was afraid that I might not have the reference. They asked me to lend them the book so they could take it to their village and use it as a reference for their reasoning. I lent them the book, and then they left me full of praises and apologies.

As soon as they left my house they met a sinister man who took them to some wicked religious leaders and they for their part frightened them and warned them that I was an "Israeli agent" and that the book "MinHajj al- Salihin" was all lies, that the people of Iraq were blasphemous and hypocrites, that the Shi'is were "Majus" who permitted the marriage between brothers and sisters and that was why I allowed that man to continue with his marriage to his "sister" - having been breast-fed by the same woman.

In the end they persuaded the men to change their minds and forced the husband to take legal action with regard to his divorce in Gafsa's Magistrate court. The judge asked them to go to the Capital Tunis and approach the Mufti of the Republic, for he might have a solution to the problem. The husband left for the Capital and waited there for a whole month until he was able to have an interview with him.

During the interview the husband explained the case in detail then the Mufti asked him about the religious scholars who accepted the marriage as being correct and legal. He told him that none of them thought so except one called al-Tijani al-Samawi. Al-Mufti took a note of my name and said to the husband, "Go back to your village and I shall write to the judge in Gafsa."

Shortly after that a letter from the Mufti of the Republic arrived, and the husband's lawyer read it and found that the Mufti ruled that the marriage was void.

The husband, who looked very tired and exhausted, was informed by his lawyer about the content of the letter. He later came to see me and apologized for all the inconveniences that he had caused me.

I thanked him for his feelings towards me, but expressed my surprise regarding the Mufti's rule to consider the marriage in this case as void.

I also asked him to bring the Mufti's letter to the Magistrate court in Gafsa so that I could publish it in the Tunisian press and show that the Republic's Mufti did not really know much about the four Islamic Madhhabs and did not understand the jurisdical difference between them regarding the issue of brotherhood by breast-feeding.

However, the husband told me that he could not see the file on his case, and therefore was unable to bring me the letter, and then he departed.

A few days later I received an invitation from the judge asking me to bring the book and other proofs that allow the marriage between two people who have been breast-fed by the same woman. I chose a number of references and prepared the chapters regarding brotherhood by breast- feeding, so that I could produce the evidence quickly.)

I went to the court at the agreed time and I was received by the clerk who took me to the judge's office, and I was surprised to see the District Magistrate and the Republic's Attorney as well as three other judges. I noticed that the judges were wearing their official regalia, as if they were sitting to pass judgment; I also noticed that the husband was sitting at the end of the court room, facing the judges.)

I greeted everyone, but they looked at me with disdain, and when I sat the chief judge asked mew "Are you al-Tijani al-Samawi?" I answered, Yes He asked, "Are you the one who passed a judgment in which you legalized the marriage in this case?"

I answered, "No I did not pass a judgment, rather, the Imams and the religious scholars of Islam passed that judgment by accepting the marriage as being correct and legal."

He said, "That is why we summoned you, and you are now in the dock. If you cannot support your claim with the appropriate proof, then we will have to send you to prison, and you will never come out of here a free man."

I knew then that I was actually in the dock, not because I had passed a judgment on that particular case, but because some of those sinister religious leaders had told the judges that I was a troublemaker and that I cursed the Companions and campaigned for the support of Ahl al-Bayt. The chief judge asked them to bring two witnesses against me then he would have the authority to throw me in prison.

In addition to that, the Muslim Brotherhood took advantage of my judgment in this case and spread rumors that I had legalized the marriages between brothers and sisters and that is, as they claimed, what the Shi'is believe!

I became absolutely sure about that when the chief judge threatened to throw me in prison, so I was left with nothing but to challenge him and to defend myself with all my courage and I said to the chief judge, "Can I speak frankly and without any fear?"

He replied, "Yes you can do that, for you have no lawyer."

I said, "First of all, I would like to say that I have not appointed myself to pass judgment (Fatwa) but this is the woman's husband before you, so ask him. He came to my house and asked me, and it was my duty to provide him with whatever information I had. I asked him how many times his wife had been breast-fed by that old lady, and when he said that it was only on two occasions, I gave him the answer according to Islamic law. I was not trying to interpret Islam, nor indeed was I trying to legislate."

The chief judge said, "What a surprise! Now you claim that you know Islam and that we do not know it!"

I replied, "God forbid! I did not mean that. But everyone here knows the Maliki Madhhab stops here. What I did was to search in the other Islamic Madhahibs and find a solution to this case."

The chief judge asked, "Where did you find the solution?" I said, "Sir, may I ask you a question before I answer?" He replied. "Ask what you like."

I asked, "What do you say about the Islamic Madhahib?"

He replied, "They are all correct for they all follow the teachings of the Messenger of Allah, and there is mercy in their differing."

I said, "Well, have mercy on this poor man (pointing to the woman's husband) who has been away from his wife and children for the past two months, when one of the Islamic Madhahib has a solution for his problem."

The chief judge reacted angrily, "Give us your proof and stop all this nonsense. We allowed you to defend yourself now you have become a lawyer defending others."

I took from my briefcase a book entitled "MinHajj al-Salihin" by al-Sayyid al-Khu'i, and said, "This is the Madhhab of Ahl al-Bayt, and in it there is the absolute proof."

He interjected by saying, "Forget about the Madhhab of Ahl al-Bayt, we do not know it, and we do not believe in it." I was expecting such an answer, so I had brought with me, after having done some research, a number of references from the Sunni Traditionists and al-Jamaah, and I arranged them according to my knowledge. I put Sahih al-Bukhari in the first line, then Sahih Muslim, then "al-Fatawa" by Mahmoud Shaltoot, then "Bidayat al- Mujtahid wa Nihayat al-Muqtasid" by Ibn Rushd, then "Zad al-Maseer fi Ilm al-Tafseer" by Ibn al-Jawzi and many other Sunni references.

When the chief judge refused to look at al-Sayyid al-Khu'i's book, I asked him which books he trusted.

He said, "Al-Bukhari and Muslim."

I took Sahih al-Bukhari and opened it at the specific page, then said, "Here you are Sir, read it."

He said, "You read it."

I read, "So and so told us that Aishah, the mother of the believers, said that the Messenger of Allah (saw) in his lifetime only prohibited the marriage, if the couple were breast-fed on five occasions or more by the same woman."

The chief judge took the book from me and read it himself then gave it to the Attorney General, and he too read the Hadith then he passed the book to the other judges. In the meantime I showed the chief judge Sahih al- Bukhari, pointing out to him the same Hadith, then I opened "al-Fatawa" by al-Azhar's Shaykh Shaltoot who mentioned the differences between the Imams about "breast-feeding" issue, some of them prohibited the marriage if the breast-feeding was on fifteen occasions, others said seven or even five except Malik who contradicted the text and prohibited the marriage if there had been one drop of milk taken by the couple from the same woman. Shaltoot added, "I tend to favor the middle solution and say seven or more." After having looked at the references, the chief judge turned to the woman's husband and said to him, "Go now and bring your father-in-law to testify that your wife was breast-fed twice or three times by the old woman, then you can take your wife with you today."

The poor man was delighted. The Attorney General and the other judges excused themselves and left the court, and when I was alone with the chief judge he apologized to me and said, "Forgive me for the wrong information I have been given about you, now I know that they are biased and envious people who wish to harm you."

I was very glad to hear about that quick change of heart and said, "O, Sir, Praise be to Allah Who made me victorious through you."

He said, "I heard that you have a great library, and have you got "Hayat al-Haywan al-Kubra" by al-Damiri?"

I said, "Yes."

He asked, "Could you lend me the book, for I have been looking for it for the past two years?" I said, "It is yours Sir, whenever you want it."

He said, "Have you got time to come to my library sometimes, so we could discuss various issues, and hopefully I may benefit from you."

I said, "God forbid! I will benefit from you. You are more senior to me, both in age and in position. However, I have four days off-duty during the week, and I am at your service then."

We agreed to meet every Saturday, for he did not have court hearings on that day. After he asked me to leave with him the Sahihs of al-Bukhari and Muslim and "al-Fatawa" by Mahmud Shaltoot to copy the relevant texts from them, he stood up and saw me out of his office.

I came out full of joy and thanking Allah, praise be to Him for that moral victory. I entered the court full of fear and threatened with imprisonment, but came out with the chief judge becoming a good friend of mine and asking me to meet him for discussion so that he could benefit from me. It is the grace of Ahl al-Bayt's way. It does not let down those people who keep to it, and it is a safe refuge for whoever comes to it.

The woman's husband talked about what happened to the people of his village, and the news spread to the neighboring villages when the wife returned to her husband's house, and the case ended with the marriage being legal. The people started saying that I was more knowledge able than anybody even the Republic's Mufti.

The husband came to my house with a big car and invited me and my family to his village and told me that the people there were waiting for me and they would slaughter three calves to celebrate the occasion. I apologized to him for not being able to accept his invitation because I was busy in Gafsah and told him that I would visit them some other time if Allah wished.

The chief judge also talked to his friends and the case became famous. Thus, Allah prevailed on the cunning of those wicked people, some of them came to apologize, others were enlightened by Allah and became one of the faithful this is truly the grace of Allah. He gives it to whoever He likes. Allah is the Most Gracious.

Our last word is to say: Thanks be to Allah, Lord of Creation, and may Allah bless our master Muhammad and his purified Household.